MY YEAR
OF THE
RACEHORSE

MY YEAR OF THE

KEVIN CHONG

RACEHORSE

FALLING IN LOVE
with the
SPORT OF KINGS

GREYSTONE BOOKS
D&M PUBLISHERS INC.
Vancouver/Toronto/Berkeley

Greystone Books
An imprint of D&M Publishers Inc.
2323 Quebec Street, Suite 201
Vancouver BC Canada V5T 4S7
www.greystonebooks.com

Cataloguing data available from Library and Archives Canada
ISBN 978-1-55365-520-6 (pbk.) · ISBN 978-1-55365-840-5 (ebook)

Editing by Peter Norman
Cover and text design by Peter Cocking
Cover photograph © Andersen Ross/Getty Images
Printed and bound in Canada by Friesens
Text printed on acid-free, 30% post-consumer paper
Distributed in the U.S. by Publishers Group West

We gratefully acknowledge the financial support of the Canada Council for the Arts, the British Columbia Arts Council, the Province of British Columbia through the Book Publishing Tax Credit, and the Government of Canada through the Canada Book Fund for our publishing activities.

"Keep yourself in

the best of company,

and your horse in the worst."

RACING WISDOM

CONTENTS

⇒ 1 ⟸

AND HE'S OFF!

O N THE FIRST Saturday that May, Hastings Racecourse
feels as festive as a can of mushroom soup. Under a
low-pressure system, the careworn racetrack is almost
full—if you're seeing double. I'm perched on a park bench on
the outer lip of the undersized dirt track, opposite the tote
board, which tallies bets and odds and post times in blinking
lights, next to the infield's duck pond. Right now, the actual racing oval sits empty during an extended intermission in the card
while the Kentucky Derby is being contested kitty-corner across
the continent.

From the bleacher seats in the grandstand, painted the same
military green as the barns in the distance, a conga line of bachelor party attendees, toting wallet chains and tribal tattoos with
their turned-brim fedoras and Hawaiian shirts, the body spray
wafting in their wake like a propane leak, tumble down the
aisle to the beer tent. They pass the box seats reserved for the
families of the owners, the faux-jolly lumber magnates in jeans
and windbreakers. Outdoors, I conclude, is for the few youthful
poseurs present today.

I'd gladly lump myself with the railbirds, the silver-haired punters, who are all watching the real action onscreen in one of the dozens of simulcast screens playing in the grandstand basement. The stout, moustache-bearing guy next to me, who smells more of coffee than beer or mint julep, is chatty like an expectant daddy. When our eyes meet looking down from the screen, he taps his program. "I've got seven keyed to four, five, and fifteen on a triactor," he says proudly. "The seven-horse came off the pace to win in Arkansas three weeks ago."

"I bet on seven, too," I admit reluctantly, knowing it will feed our bond. (Mutuel betting at the racetrack means our fortunes will be won from or lost to those who bet on other horses. Like poker, gamblers play against each other and not the house, which only pulls in a rake.) "It's been a while since I've had a good day."

"I hear you," he says. "Last time I got lucky was the seventies. I was at the border with an ounce of hash in a Thermos and they searched the car ahead of me."

"Why do you keep coming back?" I ask.

He shrugs. "Every day is new."

As the horses are escorted into the gates, I step away and blend back into the crowd. Planted there, we cock back our heads like we're at the dentist's, making polygonal, root-canal faces as we clutch our mutuel tickets. On that Saturday that May, 153,563 people in Louisville are packed together, in the stands and infield at Churchill Downs, to watch million-dollar racehorses run for two minutes. As I look around, the crowd isn't nearly as drunk, as event-attired, or as hyped-up as the people at the Derby. On the plus side, no one in this half-filled track can be seen publicly urinating.

If anyone's making a puddle around me, it's because of prostate surgery. After all, the primary demographic at Hastings Racecourse is old and male, equal parts white or Asian, plus a sprinkling of men who mutter to themselves in nicotine-scorched Caribbean English. In their fraying argyle sweaters, their tweed blazers and baseball caps, their sensible sneakers and fanny packs, these horseplayers squint away at their copies of the *Daily Racing Form*, cross out the low-paying favourites from their copies of the racing program—which details the performance history of every contestant, equine and man, from a trainer's winning percentage to a horse's prize earnings—with emphatic X's, and sift through the shifting onscreen odds. All of them take one collective gasp as the horses onscreen pop out of the gates like corks from champagne bottles.

For most of the broadcast, the pacesetter is a horse named Regal Ransom. It's only at the top of the stretch that another three-year-old called Mine That Bird threads his way to the rail and begins to pull away from the pack. The announcer for the NBC broadcast seems to disregard the 50-to-1 long shot until, in the final stretch, when his victory is nearly cemented, he takes notice and his voice rises abruptly like an airbag that inflates two beats after fatal impact.

It should be an exciting finale, but all those around me groan as their wagers are snuffed out. "You think that horse even knows it won?" says the guy next to me, tearing up his mutuel tickets. "Horse won a million-dollar race and all it'll get is a bag of carrots."

Onscreen, the commentators gnaw through the gristle of the bet-busting finale while the winning horse idles on the toffee-coloured Kentucky dirt track, calm and unimpressed, as his rider inhales the boozy grandstand cheers. The horse I bet $10 to win, Dunkirk, stumbled out of the gate. And Papa Clem, the seven-horse I bet to show (i.e., finish in the top three) was edged out for bronze at the wire. In real life, I don't part with money this easily. I take out movies from the library and purchase toner-refill kits for my printer on eBay; I buy the coffee that's on sale, not the kind I really like. Gambling, then, is self-betrayal—like being an Amish astronaut.

Hateful notions spin-cycle within my skull. I curse out the horses as million-dollar pigs, pedigreed abominations. I curse out the jockeys as pampered, albeit skilfully waxed, tree monkeys. And then I curse out the over-biting, rheumy-eyed oldsters around me who've won money—my useful, young-man money—today, wishing eight o'clock dinners and kidney stones on them all. No wonder this sport is dying, made irrelevant to today's gambler by looser gaming restrictions and more expedient methods of wagering: online poker, Internet sports betting, virtual backgammon, video slots, and, of course, casinos within walking distance. A half-hour passes between races at any track; living in this hurry-hurry world, people can't lose their money fast enough.

Of course, my sense of being financially violated is compounded by the fact that I'm here to see my own horse, which I bought with my own money, race for the very first time with me as her owner. What seemed enticing as a wouldn't-it-be-nice scheme now feels disorienting and costly.

I join the bettors outside on the apron, the paved area between the track and the grandstand. Like its aging clientele, Hastings is not without charm, but is far from its most dapper, dewiest prime. Beyond the newly installed slot machines, the racecourse, built in 1889, wears its recent paint job like a threadbare but freshly pressed suit. Behind the grandstand you'll find the outdated hockey rink and the charmingly creaky amusement park, which sits quietly until the summer, when the annual fair, the Pacific National Exhibition, lets city kids pet farm animals and eat deep-fried Oreos. Beyond the track's dirt oval, the immense, eggplant-purple mountains squat on their haunches behind the Cascadia Terminal and the ships in the port. It's a tycoon-pricey view in a predominantly working-class neighbourhood; if the city were drawn from scratch today, the track wouldn't be allowed these sightlines.

A pre-recorded fanfare trills over the PA. The four-legged land yachts float down the front stretch in single file. One of these horses, my horse, is a five-year-old, bay-coloured mare with a white star between her eyes. Her official name is

Mocha Time, but she has been nicknamed "Blackie" by her trainer, Randi.

Later, I will learn that Mocha Time likes bananas; that she has the equine personality of a biker chick; that she was considered promising, then, before she was rehabilitated by Randi, deemed a glue-factory candidate; that she earns her keep as a bottom claimer, the lowest rung of racehorse, by substituting raw exertion for ability; that she makes cheques despite an ungainly gallop. But, when I see her then, she's just another horse.

"Why are you looking like someone fucking died?" Randi asks. She's a lanky, outwardly gruff woman, in her forties, with large, deep-set eyes. She speaks with a drawl, almost from the side of her mouth. "You should be excited."

"I lost some money."

"Big deal. Anybody else who'd have a horse racing would be thrilled."

I shake my head vigorously. "If I were any more excited, I'd be in diapers," I insist.

In truth, "excited" isn't exactly how I feel. It's more like a low-level agitation that comes when I insert myself into a place I don't belong, among people I don't fully trust; among people who, in turn, see me as a disingenuous boob. I also feel the guilt that comes when I'm unable to share the excitement felt by others, because I've spent an entire life trying to conceal emotion and avoiding collective outbursts of feeling. Like during many of my endeavours, I've entered a self-obsessive state that makes me wonder whether, instead of a heart buried in my chest cavity, scientists of tomorrow will find a double-stuffed baked potato.

So, in fact, "excited" is only partly how I feel.

AS FAR BACK as I can remember, I always never wanted to own a racehorse. In fact, as a child, I never wanted to own a racing greyhound, too. Oh, and one of my earliest memories was not wanting to own a sailboat, Jet Ski, catamaran, or canoe.

To me, those kinds of big-ticket possessions represented immodesty and waste. They signified inessential responsibilities, beyond the responsibilities—family, friends, dog, and work—that you would be damned to shuck. These were items that weighed you down, even while they're meant to make you feel as though you *weren't* weighed down.

Why, then, did I buy a horse? Off the top, I should come clean. As an author, journalist, and all-around enthusiast, I wanted something to write about, an assignment that would double as an opportunity to be cool. Other writers visited war zones or camped out at research libraries for years at a time. I wrote about safari resorts and high-end slow cookers. In articles and in memoir, I'd cannibalized my life in comfortable locales. Owning a horse was, in a way, just another opportunity for self-exploitation. In the back of my mind (and in the front of it), I was hoping to squeeze a book out of it.

But that was only part of it. The other part of the explanation requires some backstory. At thirty-three, I'd run through my adult life avoiding commitment. I'd never had a full-time job; most of my boy-girl relationships had expired before I needed to change water filters. This made me happy, or at least not unhappy.

Then, late in 2008, my father was hospitalized twice. The first time, a bleeding ulcer spun itself into a silent heart attack.

My mother called me with the news. "The doctor says *it was fatal.*"

Everything inside me clenched; the pores on my skin closed. "What?"

"I said, the doctor says *he's stable.*"

A month later, his kidneys stopped working. At one point during the second ER visit, my father clutched my hand in his hospital bed. "If I go," he told me behind his oxygen mask, "I want to be cremated. I have an insurance policy with your Uncle Eddie, and another one from work."

6

"That's not going to happen," I said, squirming, as always, in moments of great sincerity. "It's not."

My father nodded, if only to make things easier for me.

While he eventually recovered, his illness left me quaking for weeks afterwards. The personal freedom that I'd fought so hard to maintain exposed me. I saw myself not as free, but untethered—like a tent that hasn't been fastened to ground, batted into the trees by a strong wind. The idea of being weighed down with possessions—if not by a family or a job—was newly tantalizing.

Stupidly, stupidly, I felt I could acquire stability—stupidly, I know—by buying real estate and taking on a mortgage. At least I didn't find a mail-order bride (check back in five years). I scoured online listings for a condo I could afford as a self-employed writer. Through my own cautious spending and fastidious receipt-keeping, I had enough pocketed for a down payment on a one-bedroom or studio apartment in the kind of older building with a lobby appointed with pea-green shag carpeting, plastic plants, and thirty-year-old copies of *National Geographic*.

Leave it to me to buy at a time when most people were avoiding large purchases. My father's run of poor health had roughly coincided with the 2008 plunge in global financial markets. Real-estate prices had already begun to drop, but, in Vancouver, *actual* crack houses selling for half a million dollars incited bidding wars. In that period, editors I had worked for regularly were telling me that their budgets had been restricted; others were given unpaid work furloughs or laid off altogether. I had every reason to sit on my savings and see how bad the year would go.

Even with all that in mind, I was determined to own property. My friend Harris, a real-estate agent, took me on as a client with the same mixture of contrarian pity, showboating, and sense of challenge that a lawyer might have representing a skinhead in a murder trial. The two of us spent five consecutive weekends perusing condos in my price range.

After drifting in and out of a batch of cramped, soupy-smell-ing condos, I began to dread each coming Saturday. To live in a place that was half as nice as the moderately nice apartment I currently rented, I'd deplete my savings to make mortgage pay-ments that were one and a half times my monthly rent.

What finally turned me off from home ownership was a visit I made to one condo—a "great starter"—that was supposed to come with a bedroom and an office. When Harris and I arrived, the selling agent was attending to a dithering couple in their twenties who wanted to know whether their Australian sheep dog would qualify as a medium-sized dog, the kind allowed by the strata.

"The maximum weight is thirty pounds," the realtor said.

"How much does our dog weigh?" the woman asked her domestic partner.

"Forty," he said. "No, thirty-five."

The realtor's eyes ripened like manure. "Could you put him on a diet?"

When the agent was free, I asked her about the office. She led me to a narrow, windowless room off the kitchen that looked like a walk-in closet.

"You slide the desk in sideways," Harris told me helpfully. "This could be the perfect place for you to look at porn and write impulsive emails."

Flop sweat clouded my forehead. Remaining at the edge of the room, I imagined someone locking me inside it and forcing me to write book reviews and press releases until my captor was ready to harvest my skin.

In the end, owning a condo was more of a commitment than I could handle. And maybe it was more than I needed. Why make a U-turn in my life when a couple of left turns around the park would do? Moreover, buying a condo didn't offer enough razzmatazz for my cash outlay, and razzmatazz, after all, was my crack. I needed ownership plus sizzle. From this criterion,

I began searching for a suitable alternative: a cabin, a house-boat, a lot. It was during a lager-fuelled brainstorming session that a friend who knew about my casual interest in horseracing arranged a meeting with her co-worker at Canada Post. This co-worker trained racehorses on the side and was willing to sell a share of her cheap thoroughbred.

Randi and I met at the track in the off-season. It was a cold night and Jerome's, the below-ground racetrack bar, was sparsely occupied. Only the diehards, the barnacles of the front-side (betting areas), were there watching daytime simulcasts from Australia. Randi, who was wearing a thick turtleneck sweater, sat at the bar, talking to an insurance salesman and thoroughbred owner who explained how one could deduct the cost of buying and maintaining a horse, even write off part of it as a depreciating asset under livestock. "I'm taking it easy now, but back when I was making one-hundred-fifty, two-hundred grand, there was no better tax shelter; I owned half a dozen horses and it actually *saved* me money," said the insurance salesman, who wore a dry-cleaned denim shirt underneath a windbreaker. "Some people have RRSPS; I own horses."

The insurance salesman left to make a bet. "I'm not saying that guy was lying to you," Randi said, "but a lot of racetrack-ers exaggerate some of the time. The first thing I should tell you is not to believe everything everyone says here. You know what I'm saying?"

I bought Randi, who rarely drinks, a hot-buttered rum. We relocated to the far end of the bar, away from the winter-season punters, where I asked her about her horses. "They're all trou-ble, all the time," she told me. "I know you want a story out of it, but I can't sell you Sylvester, because he's too expensive. He's my favourite. Riley's hurt himself before that cocksucker's ever ran a race. Tell you what? I can give you a piece of Blackie."

"I could afford maybe a hoof," I offered. "Maybe a hank of mane."

She ignored my wisecrack. "She's no fucking Ruffian or anything, but she tries her little guts out." She wrinkled her face into her glass mug as though its contents were cough syrup. "So, was your dad into racing?" she asks me.

"Uh-uh, he doesn't gamble."

"Your mom?"

"Just mah-jong."

"So how the fuck did you hear of the track?"

"In high school, I read all these books by Charles Bukowski," I told her. "He always wrote about going to the track in L.A." The skid-row bard's autobiographical stories about journeyman gamblers—guys who punched into Hollywood Park, day in, day out, like factory workers—still carried weight for me, even while his depictions of damaged women and flophouses now only induced skin-crawling visions of chlamydia and bedbugs.

Randi seemed amused by my aspirations to be a seedy bookworm. "*Post Office* was pretty good," she said, referring to his autobiographical novel about his much-loathed career delivering the mail. "I always tell people if they want to know how fucking miserable it is to work at the post office, they should read that book."

I followed Randi outside for a smoke. In the winter chill with a view of the empty paddock, my toes numb in my dress socks, I half-hacked through the cigarette that I cadged from her.

She eyed me eyeing her, trying to surmise my shit from my truth, as I tried to extract the vitriol from her small talk. I set my squint at her as some hay-pitching carnie fixing on her mark—a four-eyed chucklehead who turned people into fictional entities. Who was ripping off whom?

From this uneasy first get-together, I agreed to buy a share of her horse. Actually, there was no suspense there. Before even meeting Randi, I'd decided it was the perfect purchase. I could have that taste of ownership that I recently ached for, but also, at the same time, a piece of a four-legged thrill machine. I would get a laminated pass into a world that had always fascinated me from afar, while joining what I felt were rarefied ranks. People might want to read about it.

I would write Randi a cheque for a four-figure sum. I didn't invest a huge chunk of my savings, nor did I promise to hold onto my share of the horse beyond the year. When that first race was being run, I hadn't yet written the cheque. I could still back out, I reminded myself.

I was like that—cautious in my irresponsibility, astutely unwise, committed to keeping my options open.

"DON'T GO BEING all disappointed," Randi says, the ever-present cigarette hanging out of her mouth as Mocha Time is put in the gate. She's already warned me that Blackie won't be as sharp as the others, who have all competed since the season began three weeks ago. "She's as good as any of the other horses, but they have a fitness edge."

We settle into a spot with Nick, a jockey's agent and licensed trainer, by the top of the stretch as post time approaches. In his forties, Nick is solidly built, has curly, greying hair and a half-obscured British accent. He helps out with Randi's horses, takes care of a lot of her on-track business, including the paperwork for some of her horses.

"I'll be happy if she finishes in the middle of the pack," says Nick.

The six-and-a-half-furlong race (a furlong is an eighth of a mile), for fillies and mares three years and up (fillies become mares when they turn four), lasts under a minute and a half on Hastings's dirt track. The horses are loaded into green iron gates located on a chute that leads into the top of the front stretch. The gates open and they fire out, thousand-pound animals running at thirty-five miles an hour. Starting seven places from the rail, Blackie is vying for fourth with a couple of horses at the start of the first turn, running on the outside edge of the frontrunners, and fading further into the pack as the race straightens out to the backstretch—the far straightaway. "Oh, this is not good," says Nick. "She's hung out *bad*."

"That's no good?" I say, echoing Nick like a dweebish toddler.

Randi shakes her head. "When you get hung out wide, you lose too much ground." Translation: a horse that manages to hug the inside fence runs a shorter race than one that runs outside.

As we begin to lose sight of the horses behind the tote board, Blackie gathers speed and falls just behind the two favourites, often referred to as "the chalk," of the race. Even in her red saddle cloth, she's hard to pick out in the distance.

"THEY'RE MIDWAY THROUGH THE BACKSTRETCH NOW AND PEACEBETHEJOURNEY COMES WITH THE LEAD," the announcer, Dan Jukich, who calls the race the way you'd imagine an auctioneer would call a hockey game, barks on the PA, the cadences of his voice galloping along with the horses, "LADY VITESSE RIGHT THERE ON HER OUTSIDE, MOCHA TIME WITH ONLY A THREE-QUARTERS DISADVANTAGE IN THIRD."

"She's running okay, but she's going to tire out," Nick says, snorting ruefully. As he leans back to catch the horses as they return to view, it seems like his prediction will bear out. At the top of the front stretch, Blackie is overtaken by an eight-year-old mare named Sultry Eyes. "She's going to split the field, just like I thought."

"Come on!" I say, testing out a yelp cautiously, the way I would a taser or a curling iron.

All around us, people are bouncing around with their tickets; as horses are picked off, so are these bettors, who shoot their eyes away from the racing oval in disgust. The horses streak towards the finish line, and there's little uncertainty that my bet is toast, but Blackie doesn't fade as badly as Nick predicted. In fact, she manages to hang on, in a photo finish, for fourth—good enough for a $600 sliver of the purse. Of that, I get $60.

Randi nods nonchalantly, as though she saw it coming. Like all the horsemen I later meet, she never lets on being fazed. "That wasn't so bad," she says, moving to her horse, hands in her hip pockets. "Like I was saying to you, it's not easy for a horse to win. So many things have to work out right."

Nick hustles past her. Farther on, he runs onto the track and takes Blackie's leads from the jockey, Keveh Nicholls. I watch them as they disappear into the barn.

Flashing my owner's licence at the security desk, I step through a door by the paddock off the edge of the track, down a long, concrete corridor, and slip into the stable area, a village of olive-grey, single-storey barns with corrugated tin roofs. Outside their shed row, Blackie is being held in place by Alex, an eighty-year-old hot walker who lives in Randi's tack room. A hot walker's job is to lead the horse around the area known as the "backside" to cool her off. While Alex struggles to keep her in place, Nick hoses her down.

The horse is excited, like a schoolyard brawler who's socked his first glee club member of the new school year. She shuffles sideways on the paved road as she's being hosed. Nick moves roughly in step with her. I back away from this terrifying animal until I'm at a shouting distance.

"We need to calm her down," Nick tells me, "from all the adrenalin."

"Is she happy about how she did?" I ask.

"She ran wide, which means if she ran on the rail she'd be ahead by six lengths," says Alex, offering his gummy smile. Alex is not much more than five feet tall and is wearing, as he always does, long johns under shorts, taped-up workboots, a plaid shirt, and a fading Belmont Stakes baseball cap. Prior to residing at the track, he lived in a trailer at the junkyard.

"She was not discouraged," Nick explains. "You know what I mean?"

"What *does* that mean?" I ask him.

"That there's hope."

Hope, I will later learn, is a kind of currency at the track; people always seem happy to carry it in their pocket. Everyone but me. I'm already living on hope. Is it too greedy of me to ask for more—to have, and not hope?

2

BACKSIDE

HEADS OUT OF their stalls, a row of horses eye me down like nosy neighbours as I approach them in Barn A. It's a pleasant surprise that the backside (or backstretch— the same name for the far lane in the racing oval) area doesn't have the piercing outhouse odours of a petting zoo on a summer day, but gives off earthier, more wholesome scents: hay, sweat, and liniment oil. After my underwhelmed reaction to the first race, I figure I should redouble my efforts to fall in love with racing. To that end, I've come to Randi's shed row, with her permission, to see how horsemen really behave.

Each barn is made up of a couple of shed rows, which are occupied by different stables, each of those headed by a different trainer and its own private fiefdom. Although the number is always in flux, Randi currently trains about eight horses, three of which she co-owns. Collectively, these horses, at any given moment, nurse a barrage of ailments—knees with chips in them, sore ankles and hooves—that are related to the strain of horse-racing and the fact the animals are bred for speed, not sturdiness.

By comparison, some of the bigger trainers at Hastings, the ones at the top of the standings in the programs, have upwards of fifty horses. The larger, more impersonal stables operate like small contracting outfits, with men and women in plaid shirts trudging single-mindedly, not wanting to make eye contact, lest I distract them with my artful badinage. As they lead sweaty horses, the hot walkers yell "centre" or "coming through the middle" as they pass through the corridor that bisects the barn. Alex strides by, singing to Sylvester as they loop the barn.

"I can't talk to you right now," Randi says on my first visit at eight in the morning, holding a clump of dung on her pitchfork as she stands in an empty stall. "No questions."

"I'm not asking any questions."

"You're always asking questions."

Feeling unloved, I leave Barn A for the stands by the top of the track's backstretch. Some of the horses are galloped or "breezed"—given a brisk jog around the oval. Others are "ponied," which is when a horse is escorted around the track by someone on a pony. The horses thud along the packed-dirt course. The exercise riders press their knees into the horses' sides and thrust their asses in the air, forming a wishbone, upside-down Y silhouette. Trainers, who determine the correct sequence of gallops, pony rides, and workouts to prepare their horse for a race, linger in the stands or in a corner of the track, sometimes with binoculars in their hands. A gallop or breeze is more of a jog than a sprint, twice around the track, and used to keep a horse conditioned. A work or work handily is a more intense run that's paced closer to actual race speed—when a horse is run at eighty-five percent of full race speed.

A horse bucks its rider into the dirt and goes zooming around the course until another mounted rider grabs his reins. I see Blackie, who doesn't like being galloped, being ponied by Mikey the exercise rider. As Blackie and Mikey and his pony approach the owner's box, I nod at them as though they're waiting for my approval. None of them, of course, notice.

It was Nick and a friend who bought Blackie cheap as a two-year-old from a horseman liquidating his holdings. The horse was sired by a successful local stud named Vying Victor, who retired as a four-year-old with $537,414 in earnings and was a top-ten sire in North America as recently as 1997.

Through Victor, Blackie has Northern Dancer, the twentieth century's most prolific sire, in her bloodline. That's not really saying much. Being related to him is like a Mormon being related to Brigham Young, who had fifty-six children and today has six hundred namesakes listed in the Salt Lake City phone book alone.

Nick has a taste for wheeling and dealing, and the horse was thought to be a potential champion, a distressed property that had been overlooked by others. As a two-year-old, Mocha Time, who likes to run up front in a race, won at allowance—a mid-level type of race between claiming and stakes races. But in her third year, she showed little talent and Nick wanted to dump her. As Randi tells it, she was the single person with the patience and perseverance to salvage the horse's career. Last year, Blackie won over $20,000, which was enough to pay her way, even if it wasn't the big jackpot originally envisioned.

The sun is out and I linger in it even after Blackie is returned to the stable. As the horses pass, I notice the exercise riders, also known as gallop boys and gallop girls, singing to their horses; others cluck at them; another repeats to the horse, "concentrate, concentrate." The horses breathe noticeably harder on their second time around the racing oval. Sometimes, the gallop boys will rein back their mounts lest they use up too much energy before a race.

When I return to Barn A, Blackie is back in her stable; she's still panting and her coat is damp.

"Hey," I say, with the same unnaturally bright tone I use with my parents' dog. "Nice run."

The horse's eyes pass across me quickly, then she swoops her snowshoe-sized head into her stall to grab a bite of hay. So far, all my interactions with the horse have invited unwanted high-school memories. If I come with peppermints bought from the tack shop, she'll deign to take the candy from my hand, and I'll feel as though she's just allowed me the privilege of doing her math homework for her.

It's not as though I need her to fawn over me—that would be nice, of course—and it's not as though I've spent much time around her. I don't expect her to stamp her feet when she sees me, and pine for me when I'm away—that, too, would be nice. The other horses let me pet them; and I don't even help pay for *their* oats.

"Who do you think you are?" I ask her, trying to joke off my frustration. "Ruffian? Zenyatta? I guess you're not totally wrong to be high on yourself. I mean, you're not *that bad* for a cheap horse."

She sticks her head out again. It's as though I've caught her attention with my backhanded compliments. But when I lean in to pet her snout, she lifts her head so it's out of reach.

IN THE CONVERTED stall she uses as a break room, Randi keeps a loaf of Wonder Bread, cans of coffee grounds, a mini fridge, a container of Tums, and a couple of chairs and couches. The walls are blanketed with winner's photos, newspaper clippings, and snapshots of her friends and some of the horses she's trained. On the door, where other trainers might have custom-made signs for their stables, she keeps a World War II–era Rosie the Riveter poster. It's not so much an office as it is a clubhouse, lived in to the point where the clutter feels deliberate, glacially forged. I'm hanging around here when Randi pokes in her nose.

"Where is everyone?" she asks me. The cigarette in her mouth isn't so much like an extra appendage as it's like an external life-support system—like the portable ventilators that weak-lunged people carry with them. She's holding a jar of ointment, a paint-brush, and a rolled-up bandage. "Where did everyone go?"

"I'm here," I say, knowing that she needs someone useful.

"I need someone useful," says Randi, whose ancestry is half Swedish and half Italian. The Swedish part of her bloodline, to borrow a horseracing term, comes out in her dark blond hair and steep nose; her Italian half comes out in her caramel com-plexion, the big, deep-set eyes, and her temperament.

She gives me the once-over, from my dress shoes to my glasses. "Actually, maybe you can help me," she says. "All you've got to do is hold May."

I reluctantly follow Randi into the stall. May, whose official name is Athena Estates, was nicknamed for her birth month. She's a brown filly owned by a chicken farmer. I take her bridle and try to conceal my trembling.

"Is May the one who's got chips in her knees?" I ask.

Randi crouches down to the stable floor. "No, that's Sylvester."

"And that's the one you give bute, too?" I ask, referring to the analgesic, as I grin at the horse, whose eyes have the shape and colour of chocolate hedgehogs.

"No, that's Legend. It lubricates his joints."

I'm pleased by how easy May is to handle. I tell myself the horse and I are in perfect harmony. Could I be the pied piper of the shed row? I've soothed her by matching her power and unruly energy to my own masculine grace and sensuality, like a horse-whispering Kenny G. One day soon, I vow to myself, this will be Blackie and me.

But then Randi bursts our smooth-jazz mind-meld.

"You know what?" Randi says to me, picking herself off the ground. "I'm going to give you a lip chain to keep her from mov-ing around."

"I'm getting used to this," I say. "Do we really need a lip chain? Also, what's a lip chain?"

Randi returns with a leather strap attached to a chain. "I can't have her fucking this up," she says. "I'm telling you, if she fucks this up, she's going to be sore."

She slips the lip chain under May's mouth and around her top lip, then over the top of her head, and hands me the lead. "It's your own fault, May," she says to the horse. "I can't have you moving around. You're bad all the time."

"Is this like a choker for a dog?" I ask her.

"It's going to keep her attention. Now I'm going to tie her up. Now don't pull on it too hard but make sure she stays still." She ties the horse to the inside wall.

"If you want, you can go like this with your other hand and close her eye so she doesn't see me doing it," she adds, cupping her hand around one of May's big brown eyes.

With eyes on each side of its face, a horse is able to see three hundred degrees around—which is why blinders are often put on horses to focus them. Equines also have trouble seeing objects directly in front of and behind them. And while their night vision is superior to humans', they have difficulty seeing the colours green and yellow.

I try covering May's eye.

"You're not doing it right," Randi says.

"Sorry."

"Just cup it."

The thing is, *I thought I was cupping it.* How could I screw that up? Now I no longer feel as though I am communing with an animal. Randi crouches down to the stall floor and, with the paintbrush, starts swabbing something that smells vaguely like nail-polish remover on May's left front leg. Pigeons and other small birds who sneak into the barn and poop in the stalls chirp and croak above us.

"What's that ointment called?" I ask her.

"Oh, this is just alcohol."

She starts to apply the cool cast, a slimy-looking medicated bandage that she rolls around May's leg.

The horse fusses. "Pull on the lip chain," she tells me.

I give the chain a little tug. *I'm sorry,* I think-speak to the horse. *Please don't kick me; we've still got a good thing going, right?* Randi tries again to get the cool cast on May, but she keeps moving her leg.

Randi begins screaming.

"Oh, this is NOT HAPPENING. I fucking HATE this," she says. "If she stands still, this would be no fucking problem. You can't fuck this up." She looks up at the horse. "YOU FUCKING COW! Forget it, I'm fucking choked. Too many questions. I'm fucking grumpy now. She wrecked my fucking cast. I got to get someone else to help me."

"Sorry about that."

"It's not your fault," she says. "I'm aggravated. There's no one here. It'd be real simple if I had help."

I linger in the stall as Randi grumbles. Months later, I'll learn that the owner had already stiffed Randi on several thousand dollars; she was stressed, in part, because she knew that the horse's performance was the only way she'd make back some of that money. "What am I going to do—kill it?" Randi will say. "It's not her fault." Later on, I'll realize how this episode is, in some ways, atypical. But right now, I'm a little terrified.

A minute later, Randi returns, unable to find anyone else to help her, so we try it again. She takes the lead of the lip chain from me and gives it a sharp yank. "Go like that." I go like that.

She notices that I've been letting the lead dangle. "You hold it around, so they don't step on it and then pull their face," she says, folding the free lead in her hand. "I'm giving you the crash course. Because if I namby-pamby around, it's no fucking good, you know what I mean?"

I nod, mostly because I don't want her yelling at me.

"It takes two fucking minutes if they stand still. We don't want the cast to dry out either, because it'll cut the circulation to their tendon."

This time the horse stands still enough for her to get the cast on, which she holds in place with an elastic bandage. The horse looks pleased to be finished, as does Randi.

"May, that wasn't so fucking bad, now was it?" Randi says to her, voice growing pillowy. The horse snorts, as though to concede her point.

My first day in the backside has left me feeling more comfortable around horses, but more afraid of Randi.

⇒ 3 ⇐
WRITEOFFS

W HEN PEOPLE ASK me what my parents think of my being a writer, I fear they want related an intergenerational immigrant clash in which I'm beaten with a bamboo rod, then banished to my room to practise violin.

The closest I ever got to an argument with my parents about my writing occurred when my father, making one of his semi-annual visits to Hong Kong to visit my grandmother, got me to sign copies of my first book for various aunts and uncles. I did so grudgingly, thinking that my father was foisting copies of a wordy book on non-native speakers of English. I now realize, perversely, that I was embarrassed of my father's *pride* in me.

"I don't like your attitude," he told me softly. Then he turned away from me and the stack of books.

I don't know how people can say they've had no regrets in their life, because my life has had too many moments like this, when I've hurt the people who love me in order to protect a false idea of myself. This false idea includes arriving fully formed, not anybody's child.

But, of course, I have parents, ones who came from not only another culture and language but a far more alien set of circumstances. My father grew up in Hong Kong, the de facto oldest son of nine siblings after an older brother died as a toddler. His own father, a civil servant in southern China, struggled to find work in the British territory because he couldn't speak English. For that reason, my grandmother helped support the family by putting together bouquets of paper flowers at home with my aunts; my father once told me she had to work so quickly that she was terrified the bouquets would fall apart when the time came to deliver her handiwork.

Half of my father's school tuition was waived as a bursary; for the other half, his parents needed to pawn belongings. "You'd approach the pawn shop and the broker would be sitting on a platform," my father once recalled, "so they could look down at you." From the stories he tells, many of the friends in his youth were writers and filmmakers, some of them now successful and famous, and for a time he did English translations for a literary journal. (Maybe he wasn't such a great translator; he once joked about working on a passage from *The Godfather* and translating Don Corleone into the Chinese equivalent of Donald Corleone.) I've never asked him whether he harboured any aspirations to pursue a career in what they now call the "culture industry," or whether he realized that it was a poor bet and he should instead study accounting while holding a full-time job. And I've never asked my father—who filled the house with English- and Chinese-language books, from pot boilers and popular histories to management manuals and crumbling paperback editions of Raymond Queneau and Henry Miller novels—whether at least some of the pride he feels in his son doesn't come from doing well enough to allow for him to take foolish risks.

Carl Jung suggested "the greatest burden a child must bear is the unlived life of the parents." This quote comes to mind every year, when I get my dad to do my taxes. If, in fact, I've lived my own father's unlived life, I've done a decent job of transferring back that burden.

Every spring I come to my dad with bags of receipts roughly divided into these categories:

A. Expenses for office supplies
B. Travel
C. Drinking while on business
D. Car bills
E. Drinking while not on business
F. Mystery

In the mystery bag, I throw in everything else within squirting distance of deductibility, like an invoice for a steam-cleaner rental (nothing worth talking about) and a receipt for new sunglasses that were stolen from my car. There's another bag for pay stubs and tax slips.

One night that spring, after walking my parents' dog, I find my father at his desk, chest-high in my receipts.

"So," I say, stretching out my jaw, "how's that going?"

My dad dresses as he often does around the house—in pajamas and slippers, under a brown corduroy jacket, the back hank of his hair pushed up. He looks like someone escaping a fire. "Fine, but did you keep a mileage log of all your work travel, like I asked you to?" he asks me, flipping through his notes.

"Uh, yes," I lie. "I'll get that to you, um, tomorrow?"

"Okay. And why did you spend $900 at a butcher shop last July?"

Every four or five years, a friend and I have a big party where we invite everyone we know and serve them grilled meat for five hours. "It's kind of like the Olympics," I tell him, "but for meat-eaters. Can you write that off?"

"Okay, well, I'll call it an entertainment expense."

"And I've been through your car receipts," he says. "Did you buy new tires?"

Earlier that year, I'd promised to replace my bald tires after an unseasonably icy winter in which my car hovered along slush-packed city streets like a curling stone. "Well, no, but it's not like I do much highway driving," I explain. "It's not life or death. I'll just drive really slowly in the snow. The worst that could happen is that I rear-end another car... or maybe injure a cyclist."

"You need to get new tires before winter."

While my father's attention wafts back to my receipts, I casually mention that I'd purchased a racehorse. His head re-emerges from his son-induced pile of paper.

"That must be the stupidest thing you've done," he says. "Do you know how much that will cost?"

"I only have a small percentage of the horse. Just a hoof."

"You don't understand this world, these people. You're going to be ripped off."

"That's not going to happen."

"Why do you even want to own a racehorse?" he asks me.

Because of a lifelong inclination to try out every wrong decision before settling on the right one, I've given little room to talk myself out of this boldface blunder. I can tell my dad that the horse is fodder for some stunt journalism, a reality-prose project, but he'll see through this evasion. And then I will have to talk about his illness, and open up about the sorrow I feel because of my waywardness. We don't belong to a family that submits itemized reports on our well-being. So I say nothing instead.

My father begins to glower at me. Even now, I dread his simmering disapproval more than my mother's bare-knuckle dressings-down. My father's emotional range is outwardly narrow, and yet I feel its shifts acutely. He gives me the look of someone who resents his own generosity. His scowl could peel paint.

BACK AT BARN A, I linger around like caked manure in the backside pavement, watching the horses gallop, chatting with Randi and Nick when they're feeling amiable, or just eating lunch alone at Trackers, the backside cafeteria. I get to know people who pop into Randi's break room: there's Mikey the exercise rider, a ladies' man in the backstretch; there's Aki, the twenty-two-year-old aspiring vet who grew up around show horses; there's Ardenne, an owner and a friend of Randi's.

What am I looking for, and why do I expect to find it here? It's not as though I want to be a horseman. Randi offers to show me how to shovel shit so I can clean a stall and feel useful, but I watch her lesson carelessly. There's no reason for my presence except my not wanting to do what I normally do, where I normally am. There's nothing waiting for me in my apartment but books I don't want to read, and writing I don't want to write.

Right now, I'm more interested in making my horse like me. At Trackers, I buy apples and bananas for my Mocha Time, who gobbles them up sloppily and without an errant morsel of appreciation. In these interactions I know how it feels to be a divorced mom's new boyfriend. I may as well be driving a Miata, reading *The Tipping Point* on audio book, and bragging about going to high school with Michael Bublé. No one is being impressed.

"It must be nice to have a life where you can stand around and stare at things," Randi says as she lugs out a bag of bedding from her tack room. "All you ever do is stand around."

"Well, it does my circulation no good," I say, chin tucked in. "I suffer for my art."

Randi drops one side of her mouth, the way she does when she's about to laugh, but just lets out a bemused grunt.

"Do you think she's a good-looking horse?" I ask her, looking at Blackie. "Or is she, like, a but-her-face?"

"Well," Randi says, not sure why I'm asking, "she's not bad-looking."

On the Internet, you can find a truckload of information on equine conformation, with detailed, annotated charts that will point out the correct proportions of a horse's bone structure and musculature. Symmetrical shoulders, a broad chest, and a long neck seem obvious enough attributes, but these guides lose me when they nicker on about the angle of the hocks or the length of the withers (the highest point of the horse's back) to its croup (the top of its hips) relative to the distance between the withers and its poll (the top of its head). I doubt I'll ever tell a good-looking horse from a scrubby one—a Michael Phelps of colts from an equine Steve Buscemi.

As a specimen of horseflesh, Mocha Time would never qualify as pin-up stroke material. First off, she is relatively short, though she has a long back. This isn't such a bad thing at Hastings, with its undersized five-furlong "bull ring" (more prominent tracks have mile-long dirt tracks and often turf ovals that run inside them), where a bigger horse would have trouble with the tighter turns. More alarmingly, though, her toes are all set wrong. She toes in at the front and toes out behind (i.e., her front toes point in, and her hind ones go out). Her knees poke out when they should be in line with the rest of her legs.

All of this means she has a hideous racing form—a horrible way of going. Her knees go up too high when she runs, which is both ungainly and inefficient. By contrast, a horse with a good way of going is like a hockey player whose stride betrays no strain. Without this desirable, if not essential, quality, Mocha Time gets by on determination.

And for what she lacks in looks, she makes up in personality. At first, I'm not sure what Randi means when she talks about a horse's personality. Sylvester, for instance, has a sense of humour, while Grandy, a horse that will soon leave Randi's barn, is haughty, even among her breed. When I think of a horse with a personality, I picture a thoroughbred that collects antique radios, rides a recumbent bicycle, and, after completing her social-work diploma, spends a summer working at an organic farm in Spain. But Randi seems to value this quality.

"Does Blackie have a good personality?" I ask Randi, following her into her break room where we join Nick, who's lying on a couch watching a simulcast of a Woodbine race in Toronto.

"She's a little bitch, but we all kind of like Blackie," Randi says, lighting another cigarette before she settles into the armchair. "The other day I let her kick me to make her think she was cool."

I laugh. "Come on."

"Of course I didn't," she says. "What I meant was she kicked me and I didn't give her a smack. If you go around hitting them and stuff, they get wimpier. Most people would wallop her." She starts cackling. "And she would deserve it."

"But, May"—the horse I'd helped Randi put the cold cast on—"she doesn't have much personality?" I ask.

Randi shakes her head. "She's just *blah*. She's not stupid, she's just boring."

"So if May were a person, she would be like an accountant or something like that."

"Yeah!" Randi says.

"Or an insurance salesman," I add.

"Yeah!"

Nick nods, getting in on the conversation. "A very run-of-the-mill type."

"The best horses would be like rock stars or something," Randi adds. "A preening sucker."

"A little bit of rock star," Nick says, chuckling. "Maybe one of them guys that dresses up like one."

"The bar star," I suggest.

Randi seems to enjoy the game. "Sylvester would be a hero—a cop or fireman; Grandy would be a fucking princess; and Riley"—a horse she owns who's forever injured—"would be a fucking roughneck, fucking drinking, fucking carousing fucker."

"No, he wouldn't," Nick says, waving at her dismissively with a cigarette in his hand.

"Yeah, he would. Blackie would be a little slut or something."

On this point, Nick is in agreement. "She'd be a tramp."

I, too, get swept away by the game of matching horse with human. If Blackie were a movie star, I decide, she'd be maybe Juliette Lewis. Parker Posey, on a good day. Not exactly beautiful, but irresistible nonetheless, with a slightly nutty, feisty side. The kind of woman you'd invite over only after hiding your valuables, your medication, and your sharp objects. Now that's something I can cheer for.

MY REAL-ESTATE AGENT, Harris, and I were originally acquainted in university, where we drank so many jugs of draught beer that, at a starry point in many evenings, we left our pants unzipped to save time. In our precious sober hours, we wrote excruciating one-act plays about people who were *unable to feel*.

As I persisted tilling that nutrient-rich territory through the first decade of adulthood, Harris decided to find a career. Out of school, he worked at a boutique advertising agency in Toronto. In Toronto, he met his future wife and mother of his children, Angie, who was a lawyer. After failing to derive inner peace from turning out copy, Harris enrolled in culinary school, where he learned to make good tagine. But when he finally decided to move back to Vancouver, he found work selling real estate with his father.

Before meeting Harris's father, I knew his face from the pads of stationery that he stuffs in apartment mailboxes that bear the image of his handsome, moisturized visage beside his real-estate logo. Harris himself had those good looks in tadpole form at university, but they were obscured by a goatee and the peacoat he never took off and submerged under his beer-drinking weight. We became reacquainted two years ago at a garden party thrown by a mutual friend. We had been out of touch for a decade, and at first I didn't recognize him. He was clean-shaven and had pared off fifteen pounds from his frame; he'd always worn glasses, but now he wore them as a celebrity does—to reduce the glare of handsomeness.

"I thought you'd never go into the family business," I said to him, bending the card he handed me.

"It was hard to avoid," he said, maybe a little defensively, as we watched his children playing in the backyard gazebo. "Plus, it was the only way I could afford to move back."

Earlier in the year, Harris agreed to buy into Mocha Time with me, but he told me that his wife vetoed the decision. Since he only seemed to be humouring me when I talked about owning a horse, I doubt he mustered any resistance. Still, he joins me for her second race of the season, on Victoria Day. By the time the races start, the rain, a predictable groin-punch to long weekends in these parts, has stopped. Blackie is kept in the stable, facing the inside wall, so that she can stay calm before the race, so we head outside to buy some hot dogs and plastic cups of beer.

Settling onto the cleanest park bench we can find, Harris fixes his eyes on the jockey statues in the infield. Those painted, waist-high figurines, which have the names of horses and own-ers that won big races at Hastings—the B.C. Derby, the B.C. Cup—inscribed on them, are like what championship trophies are to sports teams. "If you win today," he says, "do you get your name on a little man?"

I shake my head. "Uh-uh, I can't afford a horse like that."

"Right, those are the big-time races," he says. "And in the race you're in, if your horse loses, they take her away from you?"

"I've already told you that." While the class of race Blackie finds herself in is the most common type of competition at the tracks, it's still excruciatingly difficult to explain.

Unlike the horses in stakes and allowance races, the ones in claimers can be purchased for a set price before the races begin, and races are classified according to price range. The rationale for this is to ensure a competitive contest. Because horses of equivalent prices race together, someone entering his $50,000 horse might have a greater chance with horses running at the $5,000 level, but he would also see his horse snatched away at a fraction of her true value.

When your horse is claimed, you find out only when a red tag is placed on the horse's bridle immediately after the race. Any prize money earned in the race that day still goes to the original owner, who also receives the money from the claim. And even in the unlikely case that a horse breaks its leg in that race, it still belongs to the person who files the claim.

The nature of the claiming races strongly encourages a dispassionate approach by owners and trainers to their horses. Racehorses are like stocks: they should be sold high and purchased low. A smart trainer who knows a horse's best gallops belong to bygone summers would race her at a price where she might be offloaded. Often enough, a horse inspires more emotion than equities. A prideful owner, for instance, will hold off from running an expensive horse that's never met expectations at a lower price.

At one of the betting windows under the grandstand, I bet $20 across—three $20 bets on the horse to win, place, and show—on Blackie. (Officially, owners are only supposed to bet on their own horses. In reality, there's no one watching if you bet against yourself.) We return to our bench to watch the horses march in the post parade. Some march calmly without any apparent anticipation; others step with spiteful-seeming unruliness.

"Can I ask you something?" Harris says. "Would you laugh if I wanted to start writing again?"

"That'd be good," I say. "But isn't the housing market heating back up?"

"It is, but what if I were telling you I wrote a novel this past winter, when nothing was selling?"

"I'd be impressed," I say after a long pause.

"Are you willing to read it?" he asks me as we watch the horses load into the gate.

"Of course," I say, turning away from him. "The race is starting."

Blackie starts sixth from the rail, with Fernando Perez, a twenty-three-year-old from Guadalajara, Mexico, riding her, in a field of eight horses. "HERE THEY GO!" the announcer growls, as the horses pop out of the gate. "MOCHA TIME TAKES AN EARLY LEAD. MOVING THROUGH IS TRIOLA. YOU'REJUSTLIKEME, SHE WANTS TO GET THROUGH."

As the horses blow by us, their heads bobbing forward and their manes streaking, I stutter back from the fence. Blackie leads at the clubhouse turn—the first turn—followed closely by the race favourite, a horse with the ungainly name of Peacebethejourney. (The Jockey Club in New York, which officially approves the names of every thoroughbred in North America, limits names submitted by owners to eighteen characters, blanks included, which accounts for the popularity of compacted names like Peacebethejourney.) The horses lock into each other, testing themselves against the other, neither letting up.

Mocha Time runs the first two furlongs in 22.92 seconds. Over the course of a race, the average time for a horse to run a furlong is about twelve seconds—a time that grows harder to beat as the furlongs add up. Given her level, at the pace she's going, she'll have nothing left by the end of the sprint. We lose sight of the horses behind the tote board. When the horses emerge again, bundled tightly like a bunch of grapes, Randi's little mare has managed to fend off Peacebethejourney up front, but that effort turns out to be too gruelling.

A horse has only finite amounts of acceleration and determination, which must be rationed judiciously by the jockey. In the final turn, when a race becomes serious and the horses that have been carefully held back by their riders are finally sent, the other favourite, Sultry Eyes, moves into second by the rail and starts charging from inside.

"SULTRY EYES TRYING TO CLOSE UP ON THE INSIDE, NOW WILL BURST THROUGH," the announcer blurts out as Blackie is passed, "SULTRY EYES TO SCORE, MOCHA TIME SECOND."

"No no no," I yelp, head folding towards my lap. "No no no."

"Oh, man," Harris says, "I'm sorry. I thought she was going to win it."

I nod.

"Second's not so bad," he says limply. "Now that I've seen a race, I can see how it might beat owning a studio apartment with a view of a sulphur plant."

"Yeah."

"Or a carriage house with a recently replaced boiler room."

"Yeah."

"You know, it's only your second race as an owner."

Across the fence, we see the jockey of the winning horse shaking hands with the trainer after dismounting. Then he greets the owner of the horse, who has gathered for the winner's photo with his towheaded family, who move into portrait formation as though choreographed. To my eyes, they assemble for the picture with a baffling lack of excitement, like a frequent flyer going through a metal detector for the sixth time that week.

Envy dimples the skin on my back. I feel like the lonely guy in the movie who walks by happy couples laughing together on park benches, or the horny dude on the beach who sees T. & A. everywhere his eyes fall. I want to photo bomb this portrait, force myself into the frame, and pretend to dry-heave as the shutter snaps. More than I envy the owner's wealth, I envy and resent the ease he possesses. The track belongs to people like him.

34

I should be counting my money instead, the $63 I make on my place and show bets and my share of $2,200 for second place. But, for the first time, I understand why you'd want to win a race. It means beating people like the ones I see right now. I want my own winner's photo, I want my name on a statue of a jockey—and I want it now. Is there a term to describe suddenly coveting something you had never previously considered coveting? The Germans must have a compound word to describe it, something that might literally translate into "heart-yearning that is backdated." In this language, all we have is "that's racing."

4

MAKING MY LIST

ONE AFTERNOON, AFTER I watch the horses exercise again, Randi invites me to follow her on her mail route the next day.

"It'll be fun," she says. "You'll get to see a day in the life of a postie."

"But it'll ruin the mystery for me," I say. "*Fine*, I'll go."

Nick gives me the side-eye. "She's always trying to get people to follow her on her route," he snickers. "You're the newest sucker."

Like Randi, Nick started out at the track as a teenager; in his case, he came to the track shortly after his family arrived from England. He was a jockey's agent last year, lining up mounts for a rider, but told me he didn't like the deception that came with it—telling two trainers, for instance, that his rider is available for, say, the sixth race, and then stiffing one of them. This April, he's been working with the overflow horses of another trainer.

The next day, Randi picks me up a few blocks from the track in her car. She unlocks the passenger door of the mini-Jeep, a two-door four-by-four parked outside the stables. Before

36

climbing in, I need to move a shoulder bag full of mail to the back seat; a box of granola bars has been thrown onto the dashboard and a box of dog cookies sits opened on the floor of the passenger-side seat. "All my friends know if you want to hang around with me, you've got to be fucking doing something. I don't do that 'visiting' very well."

We drive eight blocks from the track, pulling over on a residential street lined with stucco-covered bungalows and their carefully groomed lawns. Right now, while other neighbourhoods in the city are covered in cherry blossoms that are as festive as candy wrappers, the streets here are largely treeless. Though many of the homes here are half a century old, there's an open, suburban feel to the area.

"Four hundred and fifty-six houses every stinking day," Randi groans, looping the strap of the shoulder bag over her neck and tossing a cigarette into a gutter. "Once I've done the horses, that's my main objective, I'm already fucking tired, and then I come out here and I've got five more hours to go, right?"

Randi used to work as a trainer full time, but started at Canada Post in the off-season almost twenty years ago. Delivering mail gives her a salary and a pension, but its predictability drives Randi almost as bonkers as the crisis-a-second free-jam at the track. Her two-job day starts in the stables, where she feeds, cleans, and works with her horses. Then she goes to the post office to sort through her mail, and drops sacks of postal matter at various storage boxes on her route. In the afternoon, she delivers the mail she's already sorted, then returns to the track to serve her animals their dinners in the early evening.

To train a horse for an owner, Randi gets $55 a day during the season. From that she pays for the horses' feed and bedding. Every horse eats hay, about half a bale a day. The hay is about ten bucks a bale. Oats, which give a racehorse the protein it needs for sprinting, cost $16 for a thirty-three-kilogram bag. A thoroughbred eats about a bucket a day.

Because she runs her stable like a halfway house and hospice for both ne'er-do-well horses and delinquent humans, Randi's income is drained by the horses she owns herself, especially those who don't perform well. Like Riley, who was spooked by a pile of dirt and hurt a ligament before the season began. Then there are the delinquent owners who fall behind on their bills, people who haunt the backside like fruit flies when their horse is doing well but stop answering her calls the instant their horse is sick or not earning cheques.

I watch Randi hauling up and down steps and through creaky gates, cutting across lawns to reach side entrances. "If I didn't own any horses and had all pay horses and delivered the mail, I'd be making five hundred bucks a day," she says, almost as though she's scheming. "And if I weren't so tired, I'd get a band together."

In the near past, Randi and some other racetrackers formed a band that played at backside parties. Randi would sing Led Zeppelin and Steely Dan songs. "This was back when I was fun— when the whole track was more fun," she says. "Do you want to hear me sing Nina Simone?"

I expect her to sing raspy, like Janis Joplin, but her voice has a jazzy burnish, and for a second she's neither that growly horse-woman nor the beleaguered postal worker. "I want a little sugar in my bowl / I want a little sweetness down in my soul," she sings, "I could stand some lovin' oh so so bad / I feel so funny, I feel so sad."

"Not bad," I tell her.

She smiles. "Not bad, right?"

I follow Randi as she criss-crosses the residential street, which ends with a wire fence that faces the highway, so she doesn't have to back-track. Some people have laid out orange plastic netting on their lawns to keep raccoons and skunks from tearing them up.

"You'd think Christmas would be the worst with all the cards, but everybody's nice to you so it's not that bad," she tells me. I close the gate behind her as she leaves. "January is usually the worst month, because that's when all those financial things and shit come out, and income tax forms and flyers." She shakes her head. "Fucking flyers."

"When people write, 'No Flyers' on their mailbox," I ask her, "does that mean you have to carry that crap around? Or can you dump it?"

"Well, now they're making people actually write in."

I shake my head angrily. "You have to write to Canada Post and say, 'I don't want flyers'?"

"Yeah, but some people like them though. They get fucking irate if they don't get their flyers. They'll phone in and say, 'I didn't get my fucking McDonald's coupons.'"

"That's so stupid."

"You see how you learn to hate this after a while?" she asks.

This rhetorical question comes as we pass a fence bearing a sign that reads, "PLEASE PICK UP AFTER YOUR DOG! IT'S THE LAW!" The lettering for the hand-painted sign is done in loopy script. It is hysterically oversized and more visually offensive than any animal droppings, an emblem of the myopic sense of propriety that accompanies proprietorship.

"I kind of hate it already," I say.

She smiles. "Yeah, you don't look like someone who works very hard. You move kind of slow."

"People get used to it. I'm like a foreign movie."

"Yeah, Nick is that way, too. Don't get me wrong, it's not like he's totally useless or anything, but he reminds me of you."

I like Randi's friend well enough not to be fazed by the comparison. Actually, it's unfair to Nick to lump him with me. After all, I've never held a nine-to-five job at an office that blocks my access to Facebook, much less worked the hours a horseman needs to clock.

And yet I can't completely dismiss her link. Like Nick, I'm still waiting for the big score. I spend afternoons trying to think of get-rich novelty books (*Barry Kotter, Child Investment Wizard!*) and wannabe viral websites. If, in my mind, owning a horse is a sideways attempt at legitimacy, it also represents a gamble. If there's anything that I have in common with a race-tracker, it would be that I've lived my life in constant readiness, on call, for that big score. I work hard, and I like working hard, but have also given up much to pursue that mythical jackpot.

As mailboxes and slots blur into each other, Randi tells me how she came to horseracing as a teenager, a few years after her mother's death. "My dad owned a resort on Quadra Island and was doing pretty good," she tells me, as though she were talking about the family of an acquaintance. "Then my mom died. Life sucks."

While Randi's two brothers were old enough to manage on their own, she and her younger sister were shuttled between aunts. Knowing Randi loved animals, one of her aunts took her to the track as a teenager. At the time, she was a fan of Forego, the gelding who finished fourth to Secretariat in the 1973 Kentucky Derby and later became a champion as a mature horse. Everyone else was a fan of Secretariat, the Triple Crown winner, but it's no coincidence Randi chose to follow the late bloomer, the horse that everyone had given up on.

Randi started out as gambler—a good one, as she tells it. She'd methodically chart the performances of her horses on her bedroom wall. She'd keep notes on the horses that had finished poorly because of bad luck, and not because they were pigs, and bet on them in the next race. Eventually, an aunt suggested she move to the backside and find work at the track. After residing in the stables at Hastings (known as Exhibition Park in the 1970s), she lived and worked at racecourses in California and Florida.

When so many equines come and go in your life, some staying with you for only a couple of weeks before being claimed by another trainer, you learn to treat animals differently. You still love them, but you don't love them individually like pets; you love them collectively the way a teacher dotes on successive waves of pupils, you love them even when keeping an eye on how much money each one is bringing in, you love them as part of your job.

In her life, though, Randi has had only one exception to that rule—a gelding named Charlie that she owned in the early eighties. The horse had a short racing career with only nineteen starts and career earnings of $14,502, but Randi owned the horse in her early twenties and loved him more than anything she's ever owned or anyone she's ever known.

To Randi, Charlie wasn't just a pet, he was a best friend. When she lived at the track, they would eat dinner together: she would get a slice of pizza and take it into his stall and hang out while he finished his oats. "He used to be sick all the time and I'd fix him up," she recalls. "Seems like all the ones that have problems you end up liking most, if they're good about it."

With other horses, Randi finds them new homes when they finish racing. Another favourite, a horse named Clydie, was sold to a young equestrian rider. She tries to keep tabs on her darlings, but intentionally loses track of them after about a year, once she knows they've settled in. Otherwise, she'd go crazy trying to maintain files on them all.

But she kept Charlie around, taking extra work to pay his stable bills. "He loved me," Randi insists. "He would run up to me at the farm when he saw me." With Randi caring for her, Charlie would live almost to the age of thirty—about as long as a horse can be expected to live.

Charlie died from laminitis, an incurable disease that causes a horse's hooves to deteriorate chronically. After exhausting the available remedies and treatments, Randi had to put down her horse. She and a friend drove down with a trailer to take the horse to the vet. When Charlie saw Randi, his ears pricked up. Thoroughbreds live for excitement, the stimulation of new tasks and places, and even at his advanced age, he was hoping his Randi would take him somewhere fun.

She couldn't bear the idea of her horse being dumped into a vat and turned into fertilizer, so after Charlie was euthanized, she paid $1,500 to have the horse cremated. Charlie's ashes, heavy as hell in a white plastic bucket, are kept in a closet in her house.

In Randi's tack room is a picture of a bay-coloured horse in a pasture; he looks as though his racing years have long receded. Attached to the photo is a pink bow on which someone has written: "To Randi—Love, Charlie."

Randi finishes the first leg of her route and I linger at one of the grey mailboxes where she fills up her emptied shoulder bag with mail from another sack. Before I make my excuse to leave, a grey cat appears on the sidewalk.

"Here, lookit," she says to me, before turning to the cat. "Here, baby."

The cat takes a step towards us, then hops back.

"She's pregnant, you see?" Randi says as she crouches down to the cat, who just looks fat to me, and reaches into her shoulder bag for a handful of cat food, which she scatters onto the pavement. The cat reads the kibble on the ground like a menu before gobbling it down. "She's always starving when I see her, so I save her some of my own cat's food. We're getting to the fun part of my route, where we see all my animals—all the dogs."

I figure I have time to meet her dogs, but then my dad calls.

"Are you at home?" he asks.

"No, why?"

"I'm at Kal Tire, buying new tires for myself right now," he says. "If you come down now, I'll buy you a new set."

"I've got to go," I tell Randi, who's still crouched over someone else's cat. "I'll walk with you another time."

THE NIGHT AFTER my first mail route with Randi, I sleep easy and hard. For this deskbound hermit, being outside, exposed to fresh air and other people, is in itself exhausting. I need the alarm to wake me up for an 11 AM meeting the next day. While

I'd rather be at the track, I have a coffee date with an editor who's back from a work furlough; he's convinced that he'll keep his job if he loses ten pounds and is midway through a cleanse in which he consumes only honey in water. Out of solidarity, I lay off the piece of banana bread he buys me.

Luckily, I have work of my own right now: a profile here, a couple of book reviews there, and also some teaching. Any day, I can stop looking for employment under the "Adult Gigs" category on Craigslist. Later, in the afternoon, I do a hotel-room interview with an American rock star who's playing a concert the next day to promote a new album inspired by the Iraq War and his divorce. I'm not a fan of the rock star's work—too much yowling—and haven't prepared well for my interview beyond a cursory Google search.

Before leaving the room to get a latte, the publicist tells me we have an entire hour. The piece, for a men's lifestyle website, is to be only four hundred words long and, twenty-five minutes into our conversation, I have all the quotes I need and have run through my list of questions. Slouching on a cognac-coloured leather couch with his feet on the coffee table of his sitting room, the rock star is shorter than I expected but amiable, answering most of my questions with stifled yawns, then apologizing twice for his jet lag. He's gracious and articulate, but wears his own skin gingerly, as though it's been worn raw by handlers and concert photographers. I have friends from high school who would swoon at this opportunity; here I am, killing time. I watch him smoking American Spirits as I flip through my notes and eye the fruit plate by his canvas sneakers.

I lamely attempt to draw out our conversation.

"Um, anyway, I like your lyrics a lot," I say. "Especially on 'Speed of Sound.'"

"Dude, it's actually called 'Spreadsheet of Clowns.'"

"Oops, your lyrics are very personal. At times, they almost read like journal entries."

"Really?" He pulls back one corner of his mouth; the rest of his face pinches into a scowl.

"Sorry, I didn't mean to offend you. I misspoke. I don't mean to say—"

"It's okay, dude," he says, waving back the cigarette smoke in his face. "It just reminded me of this time I was backstage at a Katrina benefit concert. Tim Robbins and I were listening to a very young, very confessional singer-songwriter, and I said to him, 'That's what diaries are for.' And Tim said, 'That's what *locks* on diaries are for.'"

My guffawing is strained. "I didn't mean it that way," I start. "I meant to say it in a way that suggests your lyrics are good—"

"No problem." He sits up and squints at me. "Are you okay?"

"What do you mean?" I ask him, dabbing my brow with my shirtsleeve.

"You're sweating."

"Sorry," I say. "I'm a little hypoglycemic and didn't eat breakfast. I should have brought a granola bar with me." Should I ask for something to eat? It would be too unprofessional. But what if I pass out? "Do you mind if I have some grapes?"

He finally notices the fruit plate, the cling-wrapped object of my ardour, by his feet. His gaze pitches back to the door through which the publicist exited, before returning to me. "Dig in, man."

I've always wanted to be someone who could politely turn down free food, but I fail at every test. With a jittery motion, I pull four or five grapes into my hand and cram them in my mouth like popcorn. "So, about that song, can you talk about what inspired it?"

"Sure," he says. "It's about staying relevant. My first album came out almost twenty years ago, and I feel as though I was late to the party even then. All my favourite music was made before 1972. *The White Album, Let It Bleed, Pet Sounds*—"

"Anne Murray," I joke, wiping the grape juice from my chin.

He smiles for the first time, but doesn't seem to get my joke. For all he knows, Anne Murray is the Janis Joplin of Canada— and not just our mulleted Linda Ronstadt. "Yes, yes."

"So you're saying you're among the last of a dying breed?" I ask.

He curls his hand in front of his face, the way I've seen him do in concert films when he emotes, shaman style, before his mike. "Yeah, like that, except not in such a clichéd way."

"Agreed. Flaubert had that feeling, too," I suggest. "A sense of belatedness; that feeling of coming to the party an hour after the orgy's ended."

"Yeah, man. It's like a congenital, dying-world thing."

It's in this inopportune moment that I have a private epiphany. For the first time, I realize that my own interests, both professional and personal, have a unifying theme. Like this rock star, I like unpopular things that used to be popular, things that inch along a cultural continuum between staleness and a revival, because I am someone who wants to be adored but also reflexively scorns adored people, who shrinks from fads but reveres institutions, who likes popular things but not the ones you like. This explains my interests in books and rock music. Horseracing is no longer an outlier interest, another of my dilettante dabbles, but part of a family of aging glories I cherish.

I wag my finger in the air; the desire to share this insight overcomes me.

"You know what your song really is about?" I say. "Horseracing."

"What the fuck?"

"Yeah, just follow me. I've gotten into it and it's kind of seen its best days in the past."

"Well, yeah," he says, dipping his cigarette into an ashtray, "I don't know much about the sport."

"It's kind of like the rock 'n' roll of sports," I say. "The most glamorous and most tragic one. Did you see Barbaro breaking down at the Preakness two years ago? It seemed like he would recover, but he died. So, so sad. Like Kurt Cobain's final days."

The rock star is visibly uncomfortable with a journalist talking about himself. When the publicist arrives with her latte and his smoothie, he looks as though he's been retrieved from an ice floe.

"I hope you got what you needed," she says, watching the rock star stand up, briskly shake my hand, and retreat into his back room. "If you want some photos, there are some in the press kit I sent you."

She leads me out towards the door, but I stop. "I really have to pee," I say.

UNLIKE THE PREVIOUS session shadowing a postie, a hard day of journalism doesn't quite wear me out. On days not spent at the track, I've been kept awake by low-level anxiety attacks. I'm fretting, as is my wont, over the wayward course of my life.

These days, I'm no longer afraid of getting old. In fact, I prefer my thirties to my twenties. I wear better clothes and avoid draft beer. I've finished *War and Peace* and given up on trying to read Proust. The hay fever that ruined my childhood summers now affects me less severely; I don't catch cold nearly as easily; I'm able to rest on planes. My decrepitude has come with abundant blessings.

Now what bothers me is the idea that I'm behind. Friends have gone further in their careers, acquired the objects, relationships, and experiences that denote a rich, un-squandered life. I'm competitive, after all.

I stay up later than I should and after lying in bed for two hours, I get up with the intention of transcribing the interview with the rock star. I get to the part of this interview about horseracing and listen to it twice. I tilt my head back. Pinned on the corkboard above my computer screen is the to-do list I made earlier in December. With the new year arriving, I put together a list of things I wanted to have accomplished by the following year. As a form of stress relief, I compulsively made lists, breaking inapproachable burdens into bite-sized, component tasks. It was this format, favoured by obsessive males around the world, that I used to chart my life goals.

1. BECOME A HOME OWNER

2. FIND TRUE LOVE

3. SETTLE DOWN & START A FAMILY

4. SEE THE WORLD

5. LEARN ANOTHER LANGUAGE

6. START A RETIREMENT PLAN

7. GET A TATTOO

The list, of course, is a joke. As a matter of principle, to-do lists shouldn't take a lifetime to complete. They shouldn't hang above you in reproach, like an eviction notice. To-do lists are made in order to provide the pleasure of crossing them out.

With that in mind, I take down the list and cross out the first item: 1. ~~BECOME A HOME OWNER~~. After all, didn't I substitute that task with a way cooler acquisition? With pen in hand, I alter my first entry: 1. ~~HOME OWNERSHIP~~ BOUGHT A RACEHORSE.

It was unlikely that I would legitimately be able to cross off any of the other items on my list in the near future. But what was keeping me from finding other substitutions? Instead of seeing the world or picking up another language, maybe I could learn to play backgammon or master Morse code.

And maybe instead of getting married, I could hook up with someone online. With that in mind, and two glasses of Crown Royal in my belly, I notice that Linda Lee—a source of heartache two years ago—is available for online chat. She's in Toronto now, three hours ahead, so she must have just gotten out of bed. We haven't spoken over those two years, not even a cursory hello when I added her as a Facebook friend. I click onto her profile and look at pictures of her cat, her boyfriend, her road trip through Morocco. I click through all the photos of her, then loop through them again. The most recent photos of her no longer feature the aforementioned boyfriend, though her status is still set as "In a Relationship."

I argue with myself. If she wanted to talk to me, she could talk to me. I wasn't the one who moved away. I wasn't the one who acted awfully. Well, I sort of acted awfully, but she made things worse. I click onto her name and consider typing "hello," but what keeps me from chatting with her is a message from another *person of interest*, Celeste:

CELESTE: Whatcha doing up so late?
KC: Up to no good.
CELESTE: Har-har.

Celeste lives in Kentucky. Last I heard she was married to a mathematician.

KC: You?
CELESTE: I just got back from a run. What's new with you?
KC: I own a racehorse.
CELESTE: Figures ... what????
KC: Long story.
CELESTE: We've got tons of racehorses here, you know. I've been living here for a year and haven't seen any of them yet.
KC: I want to check them out.
CELESTE: What's holding you back?
KC: Is that an invite?
CELESTE: Uhhhhhh, why not?
KC: That's a possibility. How's married life treating you?
CELESTE: Well, not so good ...

I start eyeing the second item on my list, imagining a line through it.

5

FIND TRUE LOVE

IF YOU KNEW Harris was a real-estate agent and saw his angular, bespoke visage, the home you would conjure for him in your imagination would be a penthouse suite in an envy-inducing edifice of glass and steel. In your mind, you would furnish it with geometrical leather furniture, framed emulsions of oil splatter mounted on the walls, and a gnocchi maker.

In reality, he bought the fifty-year-old North Shore home he grew up in, a four-bedroom rancher set deep behind a phalanx of alder trees. (Purchasing the home allowed his parents to move into a condo tower that has its own on-call dog-groomer.) To his wife's dismay, he insists on keeping much of the furniture that came with the house, like the butterscotch-coloured corduroy couch in the living room, the kitschy landscape painting his parents bought in a Havana street market, and the upright piano where he's maintained his younger sister's figure-skating trophies next to baby pictures of his own children, Jack and Liam. I don't know whether this is because Harris is thrifty or sentimental; I've seen him both ways. Angie did succeed in getting him to buy a new bed for their master suite.

"I printed out a copy of my manuscript," Harris tells me as we hover by his grill. It's May, a few days before I leave for Kentucky.

"Oh good," I say, watching him plant his meat thermometer into a bison burger with a nutmeg-Swiss core that I imagine pulsing with goo like a beating heart.

He taps down each patty with his flipper, the scent of nutmeg making me think of Christmas, and closes the grill. "I'm sure you get manuscripts all the time."

"Well, I don't get them none of the time."

"I want you to be honest."

"You can't handle the truth."

I deserve the fake laugh I get. "Mind if I email you the story as a Word doc so you can use track changes to make notes? I can't read your handwriting."

It's not quite warm enough for outdoor cooking, but Harris bought the grill last week and paid extra so it would be connected to his gas line in time for the weekend. Angie sneaks onto the deck with two more beers in one hand. She has dark hair that she wears in a stylishly updated Beatles mop, the stringy, braided musculature that comes from running, and brown eyes that remind me of, well, a racehorse. Never having had the taste for beer, she's made herself a Negroni in a short glass. The boys are inside watching *Ratatouille*.

"So," Angie says, handing us each a Grolsch, "tell me about your trip to Kentucky. I've been promised gossip."

"Yeah, I'm visiting the Kentucky Horse Park, where all the retired thoroughbreds live, and Churchill Downs," I tell her. "I'm also seeing a friend."

"Harris says you're looking up an old girlfriend."

I cringe. *"She was never my girlfriend,"* I yelp, hating myself for the falsetto I lapse into when flustered. I'm always talking this way.

"But you wanted her to be, right?" Harris says, opening up the grill and plating the burgers. Normally, he wouldn't tease me about this, but maybe he's sore about my grim reaction to his manuscript. "You had it bad for her, right? She was dating someone else. And then she married another guy, but the minute you find out they split up, you book your ticket. Do I have my timeline correct?"

"Yes, yes," I say weakly, "but you're taking facts out of context."

Angie watches Harris disappear into the dining room, the burgers sitting proudly on his serving platter like Olympic medals. She passes her eyes over me, with a mixture of pity and amusement, as though I were a lapdog chasing his own tail. Maybe I only believe she's looking at me that way, but I don't believe I'm only believing it.

As expected, dinner, with yam fries, a spring salad, and a peach and blueberry cobbler, is so good I swear to hate my next three meals out of loyalty. Harris's older kid, Liam, likes to eat his burger with a knife and fork, and with mint jelly smeared all over the patty. Jack, who has Angie's darker colouring and wears wire-frame glasses, doesn't say much at all.

After dessert, Angie puts the kids to bed. Harris and I cross the backyard to his "workshop"—the tool shed that his father had converted into a space to smoke his pipe and look at girlie magazines. Now Harris uses it to smoke weed and keyboard his fiction. He has furnished the workshop with the stuff from his old room that had to be shuttled out of the house: the *RoboCop 2* and Guns N' Roses posters, the Haight Street sign he stole on a high-school graduation road trip, and a taped-up beanbag chair.

"I think Liam is weird," he says to me with crinkly, stoner eyes. Because I don't smoke weed, he pours me a mug of Jameson's, from the bottle he keeps in his desk drawer. "I look at him and think, 'Did all the weed-smoking degrade my sperm when we conceived him?' By the time we made Jack, I'd stopped my wake-and-bake routine."

"Isn't it a natural reaction to think your child odd?" I say, sitting uneasily in his beanbag chair. I balance my mug of whisky on Harris's four-hundred-page manuscript. "I'm positive your dad thought that about you."

"I'm getting a vasectomy."

"That's an extreme reaction."

"Angie wants me to get one."

"She does?"

Harris nods madly. "Two is our max," he says. "I mean, we originally only wanted one kid. Angie's an only child; she says she loved getting all the attention."

"But then you had another one."

He shrugged. "Considering how weird Liam turned out to be, it worked out okay."

If Harris lived in a glass high-rise, I'd envy his life less than I do. Of all of his enviable qualities, it's the effortlessness he projects I'd steal from him first. I've seen him on hot summer afternoons, and he barely sweats; he only sweats a little, on purpose, to make other people feel less self-conscious. Without being phony or slick, he acts as though he were born dry-cleaned. His own father shares this quality, and I'm sure it's what allows them both to move million-dollar bungalows.

Only a decade ago, we were at a roughly equivalent place and now he possesses a comfortably imperfect life—one that isn't exactly what I want, but not far from it. In the meantime, I've spent that time struggling to write books, hustling for freelance assignments, stammering through classes. Strain and striving clog up every itchy pore of my being. And yet I've chosen to put myself on a plane to seek out an unrequited love, an acquaintance I lost touch with for good reason.

I HAVEN'T SEEN Celeste in nine years. The circumstances of our first meeting, at an Archers of Loaf concert in a long-demolished indie-rock club called the Starfish Room in 1997, now have the unmistakable tang of a more awkwardly dressed era. (Later that year, she would be the first person I ever sent an email to.) It was outside the Starfish Room that she introduced herself, wearing a faded college-football jersey and a second-hand leather jacket.

"What's your story?" I asked her, in an oven-mitted attempt at banter. Keep in mind I was only twenty-two.

"My story is trouble," she told me, after shaking my hand.

Right away, after she gave me her phone number, that moment was cast in the burnished light of eventfulness. I felt like the bookish, sensitive narrator in the kind of novel I used to love reading—and now try to avoid writing. Over the next couple of years, with occasional lapses into common sense, I filled my days and nights with a suckering ardour for her.

When I knew her, she had a boyfriend with a ponytail who tortured her with the iron-fisted ambivalence necessary to engulf her heart. For a while, his absences and the shortcomings of that relationship were offloaded to me—her neutered helpmate, movie companion, and airport-limo driver. I dedicated flaccid poetry to her, bought her magazine subscriptions, proofread her essays. She got me an ice-cream cake on my twenty-third birthday. At times, she was blunt about her lack of interest in me. But, in moments of distress, she related her platonic feelings more ambiguously, with a sentimental gloss and open-endedness that I was free to distort into a kind of suppressed reciprocation.

One evening around Christmas, 1998, after I'd come back from a term away, she was excited enough about my return to remark that a lighted ornament on a tree reminded her of an orgasm. Later that night, we even shared a kiss in my car at an intersection. It's a moment that has become almost threadbare from recollection. For years after the fact, I regretted pulling away from her when that light changed. Why didn't I just let the cars behind me pull around and breeze by? Maybe we'd still be kissing now.

53

Is nine years, the brunt of my adult years, a safe enough time apart? Actually, it's not worth finding out. I realize this even before my three flights to Charleston, West Virginia—the last tiny plane I board is basically a mini-van with wings—where I rent a car at the airport to cross states into Kentucky. Celeste has warned me that her townhouse is part of a subdivision that's so new it doesn't appear on any maps. When I get to that development, my GPS only takes me to the nearest major intersection before the animated display shows only empty space. As far as my device is concerned, I'm off-roading in the Sahara. In a panic, I pick up my phone.

"I knew you would call me," she says. "Where are you?"

"Nearby, but I'll need to be talked through this."

"Do you see the supermarket?"

I turn to see a strip mall in my rear-view mirror. "Yes."

"Pull off on the street behind it."

I make a U-turn and then another turn down a street full of empty lots. "Okay."

"Do you see a sign for a hideous housing complex?" she asks.

"Calumet Estates," I recite, *"Two-bedroom bluegrass palaces from $225,000?"*

She sighs. "Don't need to rub it in."

The billboard directs me down a hill, where I turn into a roundabout that leads into clusters of brick row houses with beige detailing and flags hanging from poles like rooster wattles. They are near identical.

"Confused yet?" she asks. "Turn into the last cul-de-sac."

The phone is still stamped on the side of my face when I catch sight of her outside. She's wearing a white cotton golf shirt and jeans, and no makeup besides a little lip gloss. I have one hand on my bag so I hug her with only my free arm.

She leads me down an alley lined with air conditioners to her back unit where I dump my bag next to the futon I'll be sleeping on. Her place is sparsely furnished in a manner befitting an academic nomad. For the last seven years, she has followed her estranged husband, a mathematician, across the Western world as he completed his Ph.D. and post-docs. They set up camp in this Kentucky town, where she found a job in student admissions. At the end of the year, he resigned his position for a better job in Frankfurt and told her he no longer wanted to be married.

"I'm here until I figure out where I go next," she explains, fingering the wedding ring on her hand. "Do I make for a gay divorcee? Or do you think I look hideous?"

"Not at all." She's still tomboyish, with a high forehead and her Jean Seberg–style bob. She doesn't look too different from the girl I kissed once, unforgettably, over a decade ago.

Celeste smiles. I tell myself that I am here for completely selfless reasons—to prop up the spirits of an old friend going through a hard time. I bury any intentions I have to rewrite the past. I am here instead to prove how different I am from then. I am no longer a passenger to my desires, but the pilot—failing that, maybe the flight attendant.

"You look hungry," she says, her grey eyes like pinpricks.

Although I grabbed a chicken burger at the airport, I nod dumbly. She gives me two restaurant options: the colourful wine bar with so-so food or the French bistro that has better food but is overpriced.

I pick the second place. "I'm on vacation," I explain.

She shakes her head, regretting the fact that I was given any choice. "It's too expensive. We'll go to the first place."

The restaurant is not even half full when we arrive. While sidestepping any awkward incidents from the past, we catch up on our lives since we last saw each other: the bad apartments, the meaningful and far-flung excursions, the people who've passed through our lives like cheap wine at a house party.

As we speak, I realize that the essence of her allure is a combination of her slim-hipped girlishness and her candour, the immediate intimacy she can create with a jibe or a giggly expression of disdain, which often edges into callousness.

If anything, I fell in love with her voice, which is still squeaky and still trips over hard consonants—like she's got an invisible toothbrush in her mouth. Even now, her favourite word is "heinous." For years after we lost contact, I kept arguing with her in my head, getting in the final word at last. At dinner tonight, listening to her talk, I feel as though I've caught a long-forgotten favourite on the oldies station.

"I went to riding school when I was twelve and fantasized about being sent to boarding school," she says as our plates are removed. "Why are you so interested in horses?"

"It's an excuse to see you," I say. Then: "I'm joking."

"You were always good for flattery."

"And yet it never worked."

To italicize this remark, I bang my fist on the table, but it doesn't come off quite as playfully as I intend it to. Celeste, in fact, shudders.

"Maybe it didn't work the way you wanted it to," she says, loosening her grip on her wine stem, "but it left an impression on me."

The truth is, I do know she cared about me, but then there was the part of her that stoked my ardour for cheap thrills. And when I became too demanding, she would shut me out for months, even years, before picking up the reins of our fraught friendship when she found herself ear-high in neglect.

It seems like this might be one of those moments.

After her third glass of Malbec, Celeste leans across the table and drops her voice. "I think Jacob has a new lover," Celeste says, referring to her erstwhile spouse. "She's a former colleague who he would go on and on about. He would use words like 'bubbly' and 'energetic' to describe her. The truth is, Jacob always felt I was a lazy lover."

I claw at my neck nervously and try to come back with my own saucy anecdote, the kind I was woefully short of a decade ago, in an effort to stay flush with her frankness. "I once fell asleep during a hand job," I chirp back. "It was early in the morning and very relaxing."

"I probably didn't have enough motivation." She changes the subject. "So, what time are you leaving for Lexington to visit the horse museum tomorrow?"

I tell her I'm leaving in the morning. Celeste hasn't decided whether she can travel with me.

"I have a meeting tomorrow afternoon," she says, "but I can leave anytime afterwards."

It's Friday evening when we embark on the three-hour drive into Lexington, where we're visiting the Kentucky Horse Park before stopping at Churchill Downs in Louisville. Dusk wraps a purple sarong over the horizon, and the arid, hilly terrain near the West Virginia border gives way to Kentucky's rolling, horse-pocked pastures and its bluegrass, named for the colour of its flower heads when it grows tall. The bluegrass feeds off lime-stone deposits, which, in turn, are supposed to fortify the bones of foals. White fences cut through those hills, rising and dipping with the soft curves like thick thread.

After checking into a La Quinta in Lexington with two double beds (I call in advance to make sure we aren't sharing a queen-size mattress), we find a book-lined tavern with a back patio that serves sandwiches and bourbon-accented beers.

"I was a little worried about how we would get along after all these years," Celeste says over the garage rock piped in from the jukebox inside, "but it's as though nothing has changed."

A waiter comes with sandwiches, barbecue chicken for her and Italian sausage for me. Celeste eyes my overcooked sausage on its kaiser and tells me she's reminded of her husband's damaged penis. "Jacob's mohel had a drinking problem, so the circumcision was like a Zorro movie," she explains. "That probably accounted for his problems with intimacy."

I lift my eyebrows. "I once dated a girl who liked to be bitten," I offer as a rejoinder. "One time I bit so hard I broke skin and we needed to stop fooling around to apply Neosporin."

"No one ever called me a lousy lay before him," she continues. "I never had any complaints. None that I can remember."

I feel something tremble inside me, like the revving motor of a car on cinder blocks.

"You seem to remember the past better than I do," Celeste says. "I've always been so forgetful."

"I guess I do."

"Do you remember if we ever kissed?"

We're both surprised by my reaction. Celeste was probably angling for a carefully wrought recreation from yours truly, her personal laureate and historian. The best thing to do would be to laugh off her absentmindedness, but I can't. To my shame and embarrassment, the hurt I've felt about her since 1998 has been sitting in deep freeze, and it defrosts in front of us, then and there. Afraid that my voice will crack, I don't say anything. I ask for the bill and start for the car.

"I may have been an asshole to you back then," she says, following me outside, "but you were always important to me."

I already know this from the phone conversations we've had and emails we've exchanged in those nine years. We get into the car and turn back to the motel.

"I can't explain to you why I've always felt one way, but never another," Celeste continues. "I just don't know why."

I sleep poorly that night, only partly because of the ice machine rumbling outside our room. The next morning, we don't talk much as we take our complimentary continental breakfast—shrink-wrapped bagels and muffins with plastic shot glasses of orange juice.

From there, we set off for the Kentucky Horse Park, a theme park for horse lovers. Its attractions, spread over the 1,200-acre property, include a museum devoted to saddlebred horses; a Parade of Breeds; four new art exhibits; pony and trail rides; and monuments for famous racehorses, including Man o' War, whose grave here is marked by a giant statue. All of this would be appreciated by someone in a better mood than me.

"Let me pay for this," Celeste insists, as we line up for admission. "Do you want to go on the farm tour at one?"

"I guess," I mumble.

"Or would you rather go trail riding?"

"It doesn't matter."

At the International Museum of the Horse, we trudge up a spiral walkway that begins with a replica skeleton of the horse's zoological ancestor, the eohippus, a four-toed creature that inhabited cypress jungles about 45 to 55 million years ago and was the size of a dog. A few exhibits up, I learn that horseracing has been around since the mounted chariot races in the Greek Olympics of 638 BC. The English, who'd brought Arabian horses back from the Crusades, also liked fast horses, and in their pursuit of the swiftest steeds created the modern thoroughbred by cross-breeding three foundation Arabian stallions with seventy-four English, Arabian, and Barbary mares in the seventeenth and eighteenth centuries. Today, ninety-five percent of today's male thoroughbreds—there are presently about half a million thoroughbreds in total—can trace their lineage back to one stallion: the Darley Arabian, which was brought to England from Syria as a four-year-old in 1704 by Thomas Darley. Modern thoroughbred racing—on turf, then dirt—followed soon afterwards.

Later, at the Hall of Champions, we snap photos of Funny Cide, the 2003 winner of the Kentucky Derby and the Preakness, and Cigar, the 1995 winner of the Breeders' Cup Classic.

Both horses have been relegated to this equine retirement home instead of the more glorious thoroughbred afterlife on the breeding farm. In Funny Cide's case, it's because he's a gelding. Male horses are castrated, usually as a last resort, to make them easier to train. Cigar, who worked a year as a stud and produced no foals, was discovered to produce bowlegged sperm. The Italian consortium that purchased his breeding rights cashed an insurance policy and dumped him here.

My mood lifts that afternoon, and after visiting the retired champions, I linger in the gift store, which is stuffed with silk-screened images of dewy-eyed horses on T-shirts and coffee mugs, and bumper stickers that read, BEWARE THE MARE and THE HORSE ATE MY PAYCHEQUE. In this retail stupor, I forget about the farm tour that Celeste signed us up for. I rush outside.

She's standing by the bus. "I told them you were using the men's room," she says. The rest of the bus glowers at me. Two teenage sisters in the row behind us tap their watches, on cue; I later ask Celeste if they rehearsed it; they didn't. "It's a good thing she likes you," one guy in a golf shirt and khaki shorts says, nodding at Celeste.

The bus leaves the theme park. The properties surrounding the Kentucky Horse Park consist of immodestly sprawling ranch-style homes, subdivided by white fence, and pristine barns that seem better suited to storing antique tea tables and powdered wigs than live animals.

"There's sixty miles of white fence in the horse park," our guide, Sean, calls out in a soaring baritone from the front of the bus. "It costs you $18,000 a mile to paint a white fence, $6,000 a mile to paint a black fence. You paint the white fence every three or four years, and you paint the black fence every seven or nine."

"So, is it a status symbol?" someone on the bus asks.

Sean smiles. "Yes, it is."

As we leave the park for the surrounding pasture, our guide delivers thoroughbred trivia to us like polished marbles. Of the thirty to thirty-five thousand foals born every year, he says, only fifty-five percent eventually win races, and only seven to eight percent make money for their owners. A mare gestates for eleven months and is capable of running races into her seventh month of pregnancy. A female horse can produce eighteen to twenty foals in her lifetime, compared with the hundred-plus babies that studs can sire in a single year. For this reason, broodmares don't get the same press as the stallions (a colt becomes a stallion at age five—unless he becomes a gelding first), even though they contribute equally to a foal's temperament and conformation.

There's more information. For classification purposes, all horses have their official birthday on January 1st (in the southern hemisphere, it's August 1st) because, in their first couple of seasons, they compete exclusively with other thoroughbreds born in the same year—thus, a race for three-year-olds in March could have horses that don't biologically turn three until April or May. To keep these equines roughly at the same level of physical maturity, the thoroughbred breeding season is thus compacted into the beginning of the year, from mid-February to mid-July.

"Eleven days after mares give birth to foals," Sean says, "they go right back to the breeding shed and get impregnated."

"Oh my God," says a woman across the aisle, who shakes her head in disgust.

Sean lowers his eyes, in a theatrical flourish. "I know, I know."

Our first stop is Hurricane Hall, a farm framed by those thrifty black fences with a guest house built in 1765. Black with red trim, the breeding shed is a converted tobacco barn that serves as the workplace and boudoir for a $5 million horse named Bellamy Road, who belongs to New York Yankees owner George Steinbrenner, and a $10 million horse named English Channel.

Inside, the barn feels less lived-in than an IKEA showroom. Sectioned off for the different stages of the breeding process, it is blocked out and monitored with exacting care to protect the well-being of the stallion. Of course, if safety was your utmost concern, you'd have your gazillion-dollar stud hump a dummy and then FedEx the frozen semen to the owners of the mare for artificial insemination, but officially registered thoroughbreds need to be produced through "natural cover." They say it's to ensure genuine bloodlines and preserve the value of the stud horse, but everyone knows horses like being romanced.

We're first taken into a kind of foyer section of the barn that's subdivided by a wall with a sliding window in it. The mare is led into one room; on the other side of the wall, a teaser pony named—get this—Gigolo is brought in. The window slides open and Gigolo, wearing a front-covering cape that shields his bits, sniffs the mare to see if she's ovulating. If the mare isn't feeling receptive to male attention, Gigolo, and not one of the studs, gets kicked.

If the mare's good to go, then she's led to the actual breeding shed—a bright, airy room that takes up most of the barn—where the dirty deed is overseen by half a dozen staff members. The floor is covered with the same rubber sand used to reduce fatalities at some tracks—it doesn't freeze or turn to mud. From a row of tools hanging from the wall, our guide brings out a twitch—a chain attached to a long wooden handle that fits around the horse's top lip like dental headgear—that is fixed on the mare to release endorphins. One of the mare's legs is tied back to keep her off-balance before the stud enters her. Booties, like boxing gloves, are placed on the mare's hind legs in case she kicks. A cushioned "breeding roll" is placed between the stud and the mare to prevent the male from entering her too deeply.

The whole act can take between twenty or thirty minutes, our guide tells us. "I promise you all," he says, proudly, as though each of us had our own ovulating broodmare waiting outside in a trailer, "Bellamy is one minute or less. Buckle up, he's the fastest stallion I've ever seen in the breeding shed. What you want is a stallion who goes in and out of here really fast because a lot of them play around a lot."

As I stand in this tittering crowd, I am visited by a strictly theoretical longing to have children. I imagine how it might feel to know you've passed on your genetic code to hundreds of babies. If a stallion could grasp that level of abstraction, I'm sure it would give him a boner. Putting aside the unintentional kinkiness of the breeding shed, I think of all those descendants carrying on my name, extending my own reputation with their accomplishments, succeeding where I might have failed— hundreds and thousands of sons and daughters to live through. For a moment, I edge myself into a reverent dazzle.

But when I notice the camera on the wall above that's used to record the breeding process, my thoughts tumble into the septic tank. Somewhere, I realize, there's an office or a hard drive in the premises that contains hours and hours of horse erotica.

INT. BREEDING SHED. DAY
Bellamy Road enters and meets Mare.

BROODMARE: Hey, good-looking. Nice place you got here.
BELLAMY ROAD: Yeah, I'm thinking of putting in a media centre, but it's okay.
BROODMARE: What can I do you for?
BELLAMY ROAD: Wow, you're forward. My buddy Gigolo says you're in the market.
BROODMARE: I might be. It's been eleven long days. My womb just feels so empty, like a big bucket of air. I hear you've got a quick draw.
BELLAMY ROAD: Well, I've been told I'm fast out of the gate.

BROODMARE: I like the sound of that. But I'm not sure I'm ready to rush into another relationship. After all, I've been hurt before.

BELLAMY ROAD: Don't worry about that. There's a guy with a cushioned roll.

BROODMARE: Well, that's what I wanted to hear. What are we waiting for? Can someone here hold up my leg?

Cue wah-wah guitar.

"I'm really glad you suggested we go on the farm tour," I tell Celeste, as we board the bus again.

"Me too," she says. "This is the most fun I've had in a year."

"What happened last year?" I ask out of reflexive jealousy.

"I mean, this is most fun I've had in *at least* a year."

"Oh. Me too."

She looks at me. "It's nice to see you smile."

We're led outside where we meet Bellamy Road and English Road, and the kids—plus Celeste—get to pet them. We're not afforded the same luxury on our next stop, WinStar Farms. From its gated entrance, the barn on the 700-acre farm looks more like a country club: one long peaked roof studded with windowed turrets, bisected by another peaked roof that juts out into the driveway. We step into a waiting room. Inside, our guide uses a flat-screen TV above the entrance to the actual barn to replay footage of Tiznow, a twelve-year-old stallion who's won $6,427,830 over his career, winning the Breeders' Cup Classic in 2000 and 2001.

Then we're taken inside the barn, where a groom leads Tiznow, a dark brown horse with Man o' War bloodlines and four white socks on his hooves, to the middle of another draughty, spotless room.

"He's used to people taking photos," Sean says as we slowly reach for our cameras. "He likes flashes."

After this build-up, we're all excited to see the biggest money-earner at WinStar, Distorted Humor. But for insurance reasons, the horse isn't allowed to be brought out. Instead, we're only allowed to glance at him in his stable several feet away, from an angle. The champion studhorse is like a celebrity who has forbidden his underlings to make eye contact with him.

Distorted Humor nicely highlights the difference between a champion racehorse and one that produces champions. Secretariat, who together with Man o' War regularly enters any bourbon-soaked conversation as the greatest thoroughbred ever, only fathered a couple of decent runners. Like many champions, the 2004 winner of the Kentucky Derby and Preakness, Smarty Jones was retired as a three-year-old—even though thoroughbreds tend to peak physically in their fourth and fifth years—to protect his value as a stud. In his first year at Three Chimneys Farm, about a mile away from WinStar, he sired 110 mares at $100,000 per foal. But according to a May 2009 article in the *Philadelphia Inquirer,* his progeny have collectively "won 18 races, only four have won more than once, and they have collectively won just one stakes race, in Puerto Rico." The beloved champion, who still receives thirty pieces of fan mail per week, has seen his stud fee reduced to $40,000.

By comparison, Distorted Humor was a relatively undistinguished runner, winning eight races and earning $769,964 before retiring to stud as a six-year-old in 1999, but his babies, which include 2003 Derby winner Funny Cide, collectively won $6,901,568 in 2006 alone. With some of his progeny selling as yearlings for seven-figure sums at the Keeneland auction, the horse is worth between $125 and $150 million and earns $6 million a week. This tycoon wage comes even after his $150,000 stud fee was lowered from $225,000 because of the weak economy.

With the tour completed, we board the bus back to the Kentucky Horse Park. Celeste tries on the kitschy necklace in the shape of a horse that I buy her at the gift shop. "I've always wanted something like this," she says stiffly. "I'm not joking."

Our guide asks us if there are any questions. When no else has anything to ask, I raise my hand like a keener in math class. "So, does the sperm of an older horse degrade as he ages?" I ask.

Our guide pauses a moment, the light in his eyes dimming. "Yes, it does," he says, reluctantly.

Celeste shakes her head. "You know, there are kids on this tour," she says. "Why do you have to bring up semen?"

"Sperm," I correct her. "It's the proper term. Besides, we *are* on a tour of breeding farms. We're drenched in horse sex."

"Yeah," Celeste says, "but they're taking pains to speak about it in the most discreet way, and you kind of ruin it by using words like 'semen.'"

I catch a couple of dirty looks from the parents around me, who instinctively lean over and shield their kids from such crude language.

"*Sperm,*" I tell Celeste again.

6

~~START A RETIREMENT PLAN~~

ACK IN VANCOUVER, Randi tells me the ownership papers for Mocha Time are ready. "You're doing this through Nick," she says, panting into the phone on her mail route. Maybe her breathing's heavy from the cigarettes, or maybe she's just having a cigarette. "I can't fucking deal with it right now."

I wedge a blank cheque in my wallet like a rubber—hoping, in this case, I *won't* get screwed. Nick's in the backstretch that Wednesday, entry day at the track, when all of the following weekend's races are set. For entry day, track officials distribute a conditions book, which lists potential races like menu items: conditional races, for instance, can be limited to maidens (horses who've never won—in their career or that season) or run at special distances. From this sampler, trainers will stick their horses where its prospects seem most promising—in the worst possible company.

On entry day, a jockey's agent buzzes around finding his rider mounts, pairing the jockey with the horse that will give him the best shot at a percentage of the purse; the hotter the jockey, the more live ones he'll bag (creating a chicken-egg scenario). A race is called off without at least five entries, so an agent might also hustle around bluffing and puffing up other trainers to join the party.

A track steward is announcing the entries in each race over tinny loudspeakers when I find Nick, who's agenting again for Mexican-born rider Pedro Alvarado, having a smoke outside the tack shop. On race days, he paces purposefully from frontside to backside and back again, his eyes lit like pessimistic fog lights. Planted in a patch of pavement, he hunches with a condition book under his arm, restlessly casting glances about. Two hours after I awaken, his work is already done for the day.

"How did you end up agenting again?" I say. "I thought you didn't like all that lying."

"I don't like lying," Nick says, "but it's part of the job. Everyone's got a job to do."

"Is the money good?"

"Not good enough."

Nick offers to buy me a coffee in the cafeteria. Waiting in line, he explains in his precise, straightforward manner that an agent takes a quarter of a rider's income. Unlike their counterparts in the film or literary industries, jock's agents are prevented by potential conflicts from representing more than a rider or two per track (the second rider is generally an apprentice). While a jockey can make a good living at Hastings, a quarter of one rider's income, for six months, is part-time wages. Nick waves away the change I hold out for him at the cashier.

We take our Styrofoam cups of coffee to a table, where I whip out my blank cheque.

"This is money you can afford to lose, right?" Nick asks me. "There's no guarantee she will win it back."

Nick already knows I know this, but says it anyway, like a television cop reading a repeat offender his Miranda rights. His manner betrays a grudging fatalism that comes from hanging around people who make decisions they know are bad—they can be warned, but not stopped.

As with all my purchases over $200, there's an internal alarm that I must disengage like a squalling home-security alarm. *It's only money,* I tell myself, pen nose-diving onto my cheque. *Even if you lose it all, there's enough left for rent and fish sticks.*

"This is only for one year, right?" I say. "I said that already, right?"

Nick nods.

"Should I make this out to you or Randi?" I ask.

"Randi's fine."

Nick allows me to mull over the signed cheque. While Randi's devotion to physical labour is both incomprehensible and icky to me, I can relate to Nick's more pensive, inward nature. Unlike Randi, whose *fucks* and *cocksuckers* come off like exhaust fumes streaming from her brain, you get the feeling Nick holds back. I'm not surprised, then, when he says he left the track about a decade ago to go back to school in Kamloops, where he studied writing.

We head towards the steward's office to fill out paperwork for the horse.

"Did you ever write about horseracing?" I ask him.

"Yeah, I did a piece for a class on personal journalism. I got an A," he says, smiling. "You want to read it?"

"Definitely."

Unlike with Harris, this time I mean it.

IT'S WHILE LEAVING the backstretch that I see a notice for New Stride, a local, volunteer-run foundation dedicated to finding homes for racehorses leaving the track. The visit to the racehorse nursing home at the Kentucky Horse Park offered me a glimpse of the plush accommodations given to Derby winners in their dotage, but what becomes of the horses at this track—thoroughbreds who are too far away from racing's hubs to reserve a place in such lush quarters? It's an issue I've tried to ignore, fearing the unsettling scenarios. New Stride, at least, presents a hopeful twist to this harsh reality of the sport. So I call the number on the bottom of the poster.

After sending an email that suggests that I'll be pitching a freelance story on their foundation, a New Stride volunteer director sends me to Allbury Farms in Abbotsford, outside the city. This horse farm serves as a foster home for New Stride.

Organizations like New Stride, which was founded in 2002 and receives partial funding from Hastings Park, belong to a loosely aligned collection of groups devoted to salvaging thoroughbreds who'd otherwise be slaughtered when they leave the track. No one I've spoken with seems to know the number of racehorses retired each year, but it's somewhere close to the forty thousand racehorses born annually in North America. With a budget cobbled together from fifty-fifty raffles and Sunday farmers' markets, New Stride can afford to keep eighteen horses at any given time, in three separate foster homes, while retraining them so they can avoid the killing floor.

If Allbury Farms is a racehorse orphanage, it's a benevolent, almost idyllic one on forty acres of soft, undulating pasture, presided over by Wynn Bunbury, the farm's owner. Bunbury, who volunteers for New Stride, has a throaty laugh and a patient, even-keeled demeanour. She has twenty-four horses on her farm, including four of her own, each of which costs about $500 a month to maintain. In the past year, she's kept eleven New Stride horses.

"The ones here are turning over pretty well," says Bunbury in the feed room of her barn, which is airy and cool and has only a few horses in stalls. "We do not have the same horses that we started out with a year ago."

The hot-blooded animals here arrive from the track unhappy to be deprived of their routine. Bunbury and I exit the barn and walk along its outside wall to meet Agro, a newbie at Allbury.

"He's not an easy keeper," Bunbury says about Agro, who stares out at a chestnut equine in a fenced-off field opposite his stall. "He's been here a month and he's very bouncy."

At Hastings, Agro had a more-than-respectable career with twelve wins in sixty-eight starts and $162,413 in winnings. In his last race in August, the eight-year-old brown gelding rallied from three wide and gained the lead to win a race at the $5,000 claiming level. A ligament injury, which ended his career at the track, has kept him in his stall; it's what makes him ornery and restless. Despite his layoff, Agro still looks as though he could run a quarter in twenty-two seconds, and doesn't seem pleased to be in such tranquil surroundings.

The horse that Agro looks to with such longing is his stall mate, Irish Opinion, a Kentucky-bred horse who raced at Woodbine and Golden Gate, winning fifteen races and $279,906. "That boy is able to go out after weeks of being inside," Bunbury says. "This guy is missing him."

Having spent most of his life indoors, Agro paces around the pasture skittishly. "He's saying, 'Somebody come and get me,'" explains Bunbury, who bred racehorses earlier in the decade. "'I'm in the wrong spot, get me home.'"

We follow a dipping dirt road with another New Stride volunteer, Shawn Marshall, until we get to a larger pasture where a dozen thoroughbreds mill around under a covered area in the middle of the field. When returned to a herd, the horses naturally revert to a pecking order. "There's not just a number one; there's a number two, three, four, five…" Marshall explains as she helps Bunbury lay down dry hay as bedding for the horses to sleep on tonight.

The top horse is a big brown horse named Jovo, who nudges his letterbox-sized snout against my chest.

"This one is freakishly friendly," Marshall says. "He thinks he should be on everybody's lap. He just loves to cuddle, but he doesn't realize he's a little too big."

"The dominant horse can be the tiniest and even the youngest," Bunbury tells me as she squeezes a tube of antiseptic lotion onto the snout of another horse. "A lot of the time, though, it's an older horse."

Opponents of racing make the argument that stalls are intrinsically cruel to horses, who graze in herds in the wild. But there's also something about the hierarchical nature of the herd that's unmistakably off-putting: it's like high school. And to my eyes, the life of a submissive horse resembles that of the retainer-wearing video-game guy who eats lunch by himself at his locker.

Marshall points out two horses. One horse stands just outside the covered area staring enviously at the one standing just inside it. "This guy is higher than that guy," she says, "because that guy has to stand outside." In other words, the top horse is making the bottom horse stand outside *to show he's the top horse.* Just because they're horses doesn't meant they can't be jerks.

On the drive home, zooming past bedroom communities and an IKEA store, I begin to worry about my own retirement. I have neither a pension nor any rich relations. What kind of pasture can I afford to put myself out to? When I'm back at my desk, I play with an online retirement calculator, moving up my annual contribution and adjusting inflation rates, and calculate the amount I'll need to avoid eating cat food. My stocks are up on my online simulator, but the real cash in my actual mutual funds are barely at break-even. The horse has taken a bite from my savings, but I'm not faring poorly. If I cut down my expenses, the pantry of my golden years could be upgraded from Whiskas to Fancy Feast. I pull down my to-do list from my corkboard.

1. ~~BECOME A HOME OWNER~~ BOUGHT A RACEHORSE

2. ~~FIND TRUE LOVE~~ VISITED A BREEDING SHED

3. SETTLE DOWN & START A FAMILY

4. SEE THE WORLD
5. LEARN ANOTHER LANGUAGE
6. START A RETIREMENT PLAN
7. GET A TATTOO

Blackie has a race this Saturday. Maybe if I win money on her and a few of the other horses, I can cross out number six. I don't need to hit a jackpot, just break even. Not losing money is approximately half as good as winning it.

MOST OF THE horsemen I've met wager infrequently. Training thoroughbreds brings enough risk, and both Randi and Nick seem more inclined to pass an hour calmly coaxing bills and cash vouchers into the slots than cracking a program. Now as an official owner of Blackie, I feel an urge to know the betting window, if only to underscore my connection to the horse. The more I bet on Blackie, the more I care about her.

Farting around the track, I also seek proof of my newfound racing acumen. To this end, I pick up books on racing strategy from used bookstores, but these slender tomes are agonizingly boring—each one presents betting strategy like a sausage factory, where statistics like speed ratings, track biases, and the winning percentages of jockeys and post positions are tossed into the railbird guru's schematic grinder. I want a gambling philosophy that's easier and more intuitive, because I make *gut-level decisions* and *shoot from the hip;* I also have a *lazy and impatient ass.* I turn next to Randi. "When I lived at the track, I had one pocket full of money for betting and one for eating," she tells me. "If I ever get a moment where I'm not fucking stressed, I'll sit down with you and explain it to you."

Of course, that moment never comes. In the end, I decide to approach betting from the point of view of a screenwriter trying to shoehorn his movie idea into a three-act structure. After all, what a successful bettor does, Randi tells me, isn't so much guess the best horse, which is what a lucky bettor might do, but correctly visualize how the race will go—the way it'll set up. First, I figure out which horses like to go out front. To do this, I check the program to see where the horse is at the first two sections or "calls" of the race. If there are "1"s and "2"s—if the horse is near the front at the start—then you have a speed horse. Then, I find out which like to grind it out from behind. To do that, I check the program again for horses who are at the back of the race at the beginning—who are in, say, sixth or eighth—before finishing with, say, a "2" or "3." If there's too much of one type of horse, I go with the other type. And when the field is evenly divided between late and early speed, well, then I just pick a horse and hope I'm smarter than everyone else.

When I show up for Blackie's third race, in the first Saturday of June, something's awry with Randi. A race day is mentally gruelling on trainers, who've done all they can, exercising, massaging, and preparing a horse in the preceding days, and can do little that day beyond worrying. But I know Randi well enough to realize something is profoundly amiss when she's not snarling, but not well enough to tell whether she's angry or depressed.

In truth, she's somewhere in between those moods—plus, she's tired. Hastings held its first Friday night race of the season, and Randi had a horse in the final race, which meant she didn't get home until midnight. That same night, another horse, which she'd nicknamed Oldy, was claimed.

"I had Oldy for only a month, but I thought he was cool. When the owner claimed that horse, people laughed at us, but I thought he had talent and fucking guts," Randi says in the stall. She wraps bandages around Blackie's feet and holds them in place with three horizontal strips of green tape. "He was a crock"—a gimpy horse—"when I claimed him." As she had with Blackie, Randi saw the potential in Oldy and figured out what was wrong with his feet, his diet, his thyroid, and his teeth. Randi essentially set up the horse to win, so it chokes her up when Oldy goes on to be the winningest horse that season in Hastings for the next trainer. "A horse like that doesn't come around very often."

Claimed horses are ceded over at the barn. Given all the ceremony involved in the frontside, it's surprising to imagine horses being handed off like pieces of junk mail.

Maybe it's because Randi's off, but Blackie isn't acting right, either. She's quieter than normal, which makes Randi wonder if she's sick.

"It could also be that she's *horsin*'," says Randi.

"Horsing?"

"Horny."

"No," I say flatly. "That's not how she's been raised."

She laughs. "I've seen it happen."

As we jabber, a woman with a needle and clipboard strolls intently down the shed row. She carries a sheepish expression on her face. When Randi catches sight of her, she groans with self-pity.

"What a fucking nightmare," Randi tells me.

"What?" I ask.

"She's being tested."

This woman explains that Blackie's been randomly selected for a Milkshake Test, which detects sodium bicarbonate, baking soda, in a horse's bloodstream. Larcenous horsemen use baking soda to reduce fatigue in the horse; it can also mask the presence of other performance-boosting drugs.

Randi's face trembles as she stomps away from us. "The last few times I've had to do a Milkshake Test, the horses fucking sucked," she says when she turns back.

"I did two tests last night," says the track attendant, who lets herself into the stall, "and both horses won."

"I'm ready to shoot myself."

Randi fantasizes about suicide on an hourly basis. It's a release valve for her that's turned when the day's going badly or a horse runs poorly—or when someone in the shed row screws up—and belongs in the same vein of hyperbole that lets her call her beloved horses pigs and bitches. Other times, she speaks about her self-inflicted demise with the same wishful relish that other people might describe quitting their jobs and moving to Mexico. It's both a faraway fantasy and a last resort.

WE STAY NEAR Randi's regular spot to watch the races, at one of the picnic tables across from the tote board. Blackie, in a blue saddle cloth and with jockey Fernando Perez on her, starts third from the rail. Midway through the top stretch the favourite horse, a brown mare named Angel Came Down, takes a length-and-a-half lead. (A length is about a fifth of a second.) Blackie's second and in good position, near the rail by the first quarter mile, followed closely by two other favourites.

"THEY'RE MIDWAY DOWN THE BACKSTRETCH AND ANGEL CAME DOWN HAS THE RAIL AND THE LEAD BY THE HALF," says the announcer. "MOCHA TIME IS SECOND BY THREE-QUARTERS OF A LENGTH. GRAYROSS GAL IS THIRD."

Blackie's trying hard and staying in the race, but maybe Randi's pessimism has affected me, because I never feel she'll win. On the backstretch, Perez puts the stick on her, but she doesn't take the cue. She and Grayross Gal, a nine-year-old bay mare, duke it out for second, but Angel Came Down is never threatened. She breaks ahead down the lane, two-three-four-five lengths ahead of Blackie, who sits second from wire to wire. Grayross Gal and another mare named Mystic Pass, who's made a late surge, vie for third.

"Something wasn't right about her," Randi says to Nick.

"She wasn't digging like she normally does," Nick says.

The race had set up the way Randi wanted it to, with Blackie near the front where she's happy, but it had set up *even better* for Angel Came Down, a speed horse who was never really challenged early in the contest and used her untapped reserve of energy to pull away for the easy victory after the final turn.

Again, I wince bitterly as the winner's photo is staged. But my disappointment with the race is forestalled because of the triactor bet I hold. (A triactor or triacta is a bet that picks the first three finishers in a race in correct order.) The sign on the tote board says "photo finish," but from where we were standing it looked like Grayross Gal withstood the late rally by Mystic Pass—which means I'm holding a big-for-me payout.

This is when my luck turns as a gambler. This is when my time communing with thoroughbreds in the barn pays off. *I'm no longer a dilettante now,* I tell myself. *My horse loves me now. I am handsome.* This is when I prove myself a man.

As the final results light up to show Mystic Pass in third, I let out a yelp, *"No-ow-ooh!"* the kind of squeaky, bathetic howl that leaves a fourteen-year-old's mouth when his kid brother rips the corner off his favourite comic book. Randi and Nick wince.

I'm ready to shoot myself.

⋙ 7 ⋘

DINK-CLEANING DAY

ARLIER THAT SPRING, Alex, the eighty-year-old hot walker, did one-arm push-ups on a local TV news broadcast, in an instalment of a long-running segment that focuses on human-interest stories. Whenever I bring friends to the track and mention his TV appearance, Alex proudly drops to the ground and begins levering himself up with his right arm. I know it's bad to do that to him, but along with letting kids feed carrots to Blackie, it's a highlight of the tour I give.

In the shed row, Alex is either dead silent or talks *a lot*. When he does feel chatty, he'll yoke his life story with elements drawn from a dreamier precinct of his mind. A story might, at first, concern his previous career as a welder—plausible enough— but it will weave into his other, much less plausible, career as a criminologist and the cops who are still chasing after him. Or he'll let it be known that he once lived by the dump with his son, who's now twenty and works at the harness-racing track, until they were forcibly evicted by the Taliban. His stories unspool from one digression into another, until you forget where he began and fear he'll never end.

Today, he's showing me how to hot walk Sylvester. "Sylvester isn't that high-grade class of horse, but what he does have is heart; he loves Randi and he loves me walking him," Alex tells me, holding Sylvester after a gallop while Randi hoses the horse down. Sylvester rubs his head up against Alex, whose feet slide back. Alex turns a shoulder towards the horse and leans into him.

"You can put the lip chain on him," Randi says, "so he don't fuck around."

"All he's doing is nuzzling," Alex says. "I don't mind."

Randi's often impatient with Alex and his requests for extra money for betting, but now she laughs. "Alex loves Sylvester."

The horse flicks the water from his back like a dog stepping out of a lake.

Afterwards, Alex hands the lead to me as I take the horse outside the barn. "If you give him the knob, he'll chew on it," he says, letting the horse gnaw on the end of the leather lead. "All in all, anything he wants to do, he'll probably do it. So just let him have a little rope, like fishing."

Sylvester's shoes click against the pavement. The six-year-old gelding is actually easier to lead than my parents' nine-year-old Labrador, though I feel like I'm driving a boat or my dad's old gigantic, second-hand Mercedes—my sense of control is only provisional, almost dream-like. "If you want him going this way, you push his head over this way," Alex says, before gently nudging the horse to the right. "And when you want him to come that way, you make a wide turn, because he's a big horse." North American racehorses, in fact, spend almost their entire lives going left, from the racing oval to their hot walking routes; going right becomes counter-instinctual.

The horse stops to look inside a bin filled with recycled cardboard. "And sometimes we stand here and look at that sun and the way you're going now we'll just walk and the sun will just cook him on all sides."

We walk around the stable towards the tack shop and loop back. Sylvester stops at a pile of horse dung. Alex laughs. "Oh, he likes to smell the turds," he tells me. "Now he can tell if it's a female horse or a male horse, or if there's drugs."

As we head back to Sylvester's stall, Alex takes the leads from me and gently ushers the horse back inside. I stroke the horse's neck, grateful that he didn't exploit my sense of terror. "Now you're a horseman," he tells me. "Wasn't that easy?"

"You're a good teacher," I say.

"Well, you're a good student."

ON THE DAY I walk Sylvester, I run into an old friend in the backside. It's been seven or eight years since I last saw Kulwant, and it takes me a moment to recognize him even though he doesn't look any different. He's still slender, bearded, and tall, with a prideful, rude-cum-shy demeanour. When I finally place him in this unlikely context, I flinch, unsure of his reaction. He's in a plaid work shirt, faded jeans, and has a bridle looped around one shoulder. Behind his wire-frame glasses, his eyes chew through me like a sewing machine.

"What the hell brings you here?" he asks me. "Is there a creative writing class for jockeys?"

Some explanation ensues before I ask him whether he works in the stables.

"No, I only live here," he says. "Actually, I make my living as a banker."

Kulwant has been a groom for three years and is one of the two hundred or so stable hands, including Alex, who live alongside the thousand or so horses in the backside like dorm mates. The tack rooms they occupy are clean, rent-free, and come equipped with complimentary cable, but are no one's first-choice digs. Working at the track, of course, is no one's first-choice job. A groom's tasks are physically taxing, require early hours, take up six days a week, and pay, depending on your experience, anywhere between $2,000 and $3,000 per month. During the off-season, when Kulwant goes on Employment Insurance, he lives off even less.

In first-year university, we briefly played together in a band before he dropped out after a single term to live on a commune in Oregon. He moved to Montreal and toured extensively throughout Europe and Australia as a drummer in a klezmer rock collective. The last time I heard from him, in 2003, he was in Berlin, taking on freelance carpentry work between sets at open-mike nights. Whenever his wayward life led him back into town, we would go for a beer. Each time, he would push a new CD in my pocket and make fun of my clothes. As we speak, he digs his hands in his pockets and rocks on his heels, as though he were desperate to leave.

"Can I buy you a coffee?" I ask. "You can tell me about your music."

"I hate to disappoint you, but I'm on my way to a *black-tie fundraiser*," he says. "But I was planning to leave the fairground on Saturday night. Take me somewhere professional writers go, with beers in foreign languages."

I jab my finger skywards. "I know just the place."

"Sure you do. Nice shoes, by the way."

We arrange to meet at a Belgian alehouse at 7 PM, because Kulwant works mornings. But he arrives half an hour late. "Sorry," he says, taking the stool next to mine. "All the places in the area look exactly like the others. You live around here, right?"

Our first two rounds are spent discussing the album he's saving money to make, a track-by-track response to Woody Guthrie's *Dust Bowl Ballads*. "The recording technology is cheap, but I want to buy a van. I hated the last girl I dated but we stayed together because she owned a Volkswagen minibus. Then she sold it," he explains. "I also want to pay my lap-steel guy. And, thus, I exploit myself to keep him from getting exploited."

"Is your job that bad?" I ask.

Kulwant shrugs and lets me buy another round. He works with six horses, cleaning their stalls and brushing them, then walking them after they run. "Not bad so far as shit-work goes," he says. "Would you want to live in a tack room instead of a van?"

"Well, neither. That's why I write three hundred words on new slow cookers," I say. "That's why I teach part-time."

He draws back the $11 beer. "Exactly, at least I do something honest."

If we were drinking anything else, I'd have probably left after this remark. Belgian Trappist ale, however, goes down like beer but has the alcohol content of fortified wine. The night has already begun to assume a dissolute momentum, and it's not too long until we're ordering a couple more rounds, with an order of *moules frites*. Soon enough, respectable patrons have left, the chairs are upturned, and the now-you're-ugly lights are hastily undimmed.

"You want me to call a cab?" I ask, staggering from the bar like a gigantic, B-movie lizard. "I don't know if any buses are still running."

"How far do you live from here?" he asks. "I don't have cash for a cab."

I hesitate to answer. For many years, Kulwant was the ruthlessly funny, tirelessly anguished friend I had to please. He was the one who gave me the flummoxing books and albums that eventually forged my tastes. He was the one I routinely let down with my concessions to the imperatives of convention and comfort. When I decided to let someone else disappoint him, it took only two unanswered emails to deflect him from my social orbit. His default bitterness makes it hard to tell whether he's sore with me, so I'm thrown off by his request to crash at my place.

Eventually, we stumble fifteen blocks to my apartment. I've been at the same address for six years now. It's filled with cheap furniture, used books on every horizontal surface, and an area rug that I bought at Costco for $30. I've stayed so long because the place is central, not too far east or too far west, not too far from my parents—geographically ambivalent, how fitting.

Kulwant settles back on my IKEA couch as I bring him a glass of water. Normally, when guests see my place, I figure they're making mental calculations, imagining the set of bad decisions necessary to bring someone with a solid upbringing to these circumstances. But I can tell that Kulwant, who also lives where he works, is doing that math on himself. My apartment compares favourably to his tack room. That look of unrestrained envy on his face makes up for the bar tab I covered.

"So how many Crock-Pots do you need to sell to live here?" he asks, after he downs his water in two messy gulps.

I pull out the cot from my closet, and then head to the washroom. "Not as many as you think," I say. "I'm only a renter."

"At least you're not that guy Harris. Remember him? You will never believe what he's doing for a living."

"Well, his dad sold real estate, too," I say from the bathroom sink, where I'm brushing my teeth.

"That guy sold his soul. You've just leased yours out."

When I re-emerge from my bedtime ablutions, Kulwant is sitting on the cot, stripped down to his underwear.

"You need to be up at dawn, right?" I ask. "Should I set an alarm?"

"These days I get up without any help. I sleepwalk into the stalls," he says. "Do you remember the time I peed on you?"

"Uh-huh," I say.

It was back in the nineties when Kulwant lived in an attic apartment, above a deaf woman who didn't mind loud music. I was on the couch of his two-room place and he was so drunk that he mistook my head for the toilet bowl. Fortunately, I covered my face with his comforter—which I continued to sleep under until I woke up three hours later.

My bed fits into a windowless nook, five feet from my toilet. That night, it takes me longer than usual to nod off—I'm half-expecting to be Kulwant's latrine—but at some point, I'm so exhausted that I stop worrying about it. When I rise in the morning, Kulwant is already gone, the bedding folded neatly on my couch, leaving only the impression of his hairy form on the empty cot and a CD of his newest songs.

"CLEANING DINKS WAS one of the first things I learned as a groom," Randi tells me, lugging the bucket that she uses to wash horse penises down the shed row to another trainer's stable. "Nowadays, people don't have enough time."

In his stall at the track, lying on bedding, a male horse will collect dirt, scum, and sawdust in his nether regions. After a few months, the horse penis, which retracts into a sheath, becomes a smegma factory, which leads to infection, discomfort, and difficulties with urination. Cleaning a horse penis is a straightforward, if unsavoury task that many of today's newfangled grooms are too icked out to perform. At the same time, handling a thousand-pound animal's junk requires confidence and finesse; a bold novice might get himself hurt if he squeezes or pulls too hard.

"You have to fucking have a knack for it," Randi tells me. "You have to be gentle."

When other trainers found out that Randi was willing to do the work, it became a lucrative part-time job for her—at $20 a go, cleaning half a dozen horse penises at a time. Randi even had joke business cards made:

> **SWEARING RANDI'S**
> **DINK-CLEANING SERVICE**
>
> ─────────
>
> *Smegma is my specialty*

Once we get to the other barn, Randi introduces me to a groom named Daryl, a friendly guy wearing a baseball cap over his mullet, who holds the horses while Randi roots underneath them.

The first horse, a four-year-old named Surprisal, lets Randi give him the reach-around with little apprehension. Randi uses soap and a sponge, though some of the horse-care websites I visit afterwards also suggest using K-Y Jelly. She leans under him with her free hand dangling back for balance as though she were fencing.

"He's not very dirty," Randi says, turning to me with an almost disappointed look. "I've done him a few times before."

Like many horses at Hastings whose bloodlines aren't worth passing on, Surprisal is gelded. An unaltered horse brings another degree of awkwardness to dink cleaning. Randi, who's taken a week off from the post office, says that she cleaned a ball-swinging colt the day before. "He kind of liked it, which can make the job easier," Randi says, breaking into a smile. "Usually, when they're studs, they're real jerks."

But I won't get to see Randi clean an unaltered horse this afternoon; dreams don't always come true. The next thoroughbred on her list, a two-year-old named TJ, has never had his business cleaned before. "Are you ready, little dude?" she says to him. "Don't kick me."

Randi reaches down and the horse is so startled he hops back, splaying his hind legs. Randi tells me to stand back, in case she's forced to jump out of the stall. Some horses behave so badly when their penises are cleaned that they need to be tranquilized. Eventually, though, TJ settles down. Maybe it's the classic-rock station on the shed row radio playing AC/DC's "You Shook Me All Night Long" that soothes him.

"When they're two, they're like teenagers in human years," I suggest.

"They're more like eight-year-old kids," Randi says. "They're still willing to learn."

Daryl nods in agreement. "They're adolescents."

"Look at this shit," she says, showing me some of the gunk that she's cleaned from the shaft of the horse's penis.

Both Daryl and I groan in disgust. "It looks like burnt cheese," I tell her.

"That's why they pay me the big bucks," she says, before leaning back in. "Now I'm going to go for the bean."

The bean is the name for the hard lump of smegma that builds up on the tip of the horse's urethra—where he pees. Randi pulls out TJ's bean and holds it for me to inspect like the prize inside the chocolate egg.

"It's white and bent," I say. "It's like a cashew."

Randi laughs. "You're good at describing things."

"Yes, I have the most useless talents."

The biggest challenge of the afternoon is a big four-year-old named Tex who's never had his dink cleaned before. He pins his ears back—normally the sign of an angry horse—when Randi reaches down.

"She's putting her life in his hands," says Daryl, who's not sure I appreciate the skill involved. "When they tense up, she backs off. You have to do it by feel."

"People who read books on this stuff don't know a fucking thing," Randi says. "No offence to you."

I don't take this comment personally, but instead wince as she reaches inside the horse's sheath, digging in there as though she's looking for loose change in her car seat. As though by special request, the classic-rock station is now playing "Dazed and Confused" by Led Zeppelin. Robert Plant singing about how he "wanted a woman but never bargained for you," then moaning like a cat with acid reflux might just be the perfect soundtrack for a female trainer cleaning a horse's penis.

"How old are they when they're gelded?" I ask Daryl.

"Some when they're two, some earlier," he says. "It's not that hard. I've done cows and pigs. You cut it open with a scalpel and remove it. You use a local anaesthetic and tranq them."

"Then once it's done," Randi says, "you hose them and get them outside. You might think it's mean, but they're worse doing nothing. They need to keep moving, get the blood flowing down there."

Randi pulls out another bean. "Look at the size of that one," she says, holding it in her palm. "How would you like that in the middle of your dink?"

"Awwwwgggh," I groan.

"Squeeze it."

She drops the bean in my palm and I reluctantly pinch it with my thumb and middle finger.

"It has a spongy texture," I say, starting to feel like the horse-smegma equivalent of a wine taster, "like a recently used ear plug."

"Heh," she says. "I've got another."

"I don't need—"

"Here."

She places it in my hand. "It looks like a clove of garlic," I say.

At first, I drop it on the bedding floor, but after thinking about it, I retrieve it and wrap it in tissue paper. "I'm going to gross out my friends with this at the bar," I say, which makes Randi laugh.

That night, I gross everyone out.

➤ 8 ⟵

HAPPY VALLEY

As I tell this story, it occurs to me that my decision to buy a racehorse may have also been influenced by a family trip I took to Hong Kong, where I visited Happy Valley Racecourse. It happened in March, only two months before I met Mocha Time.

I hadn't visited the city of my birth in seventeen years, and my dad, who wanted me to see my ninety-six-year-old grandmother, offered to pay for my flight. The day before our trip to the track, we visited her. At dim sum with my Ninth Uncle—my Dad belongs to one of those bulk-quantity families that people, paradoxically, only have when they're poor—she told me, as she did whenever my father passed the phone to me in Canada, that my Cantonese had improved. (In reality, I speak my mother tongue like a toddler who'd been deprived of oxygen at birth. It was out of embarrassment that it had taken so long to return.) After the meal, we followed my grandmother's Filipina helper, pushing my grandmother in her wheelchair, into the apartment they share with my uncle and his family.

As I looked out the window to the courtyard pool, my father called me into my grandmother's room. "You have to see this," he insisted.

Her bedroom—in less cramped cities, it would be a den or a storage room—is covered with photos. On a dresser she keeps a photo of her husband, my grandfather, when he's not much older than I was then. He wears a speckled bow tie and has a thick, doughy face. It's the same photo that's been on the fireplace mantle of my parents' house since I was a child. The most prominent photo in her room, though, is a framed family portrait taken about twenty years ago in Vancouver when my grandmother, whose short-term memory is failing, crossed the ocean to visit the half of her family that was then living in Canada. (Some moved back after acquiring their Canadian passports.) It was taken so long ago I don't even remember being part of the photo. There are about two dozen of us—my grandmother, the root of our family, seated in the centre. I'm in the back row, a fourteen-year-old in an X-Pensive Winos T-shirt; the rest of my cousins are in sweaters and button-up shirts or dresses.

Along the edges of the photo, and in the foreground, she's cut out pictures of her other children, grandchildren, and great-grandchildren—some of whom weren't born when the original portrait was taken—and pasted them into the scene, scrapbook-style, to create a composite portrait of her entire far-flung brood.

"Isn't your grandmother clever?" my mother asked, pointing to one of the pasted-on pictures.

While she received this praise graciously, my grandmother still seemed shrewd enough to recognize this well-meaning condescension for what it was.

We made plans for dinner later that week, then let my father's mother rest. On the elevator ride down, my father asked whether I still wanted to see the Wednesday night races.

"Haven't you been running around enough?" my mother asked him. "You could easily take tomorrow night off."

My father looked annoyed. "I don't feel tired at all."

To my mother's consternation, my father made no attempt to reserve his energy on our trip despite his tenuous health. He would outpace me on our excursions while pointing out nostalgic sights in passing, like the old bank he used to manage, the department store my First Aunt worked in where she met her husband, and the Lutheran school where he taught English. Invoking these personal landmarks, selling the city of his youth to me, he came off as the one who hadn't visited in seventeen years.

As we stepped out of the elevator, my father's phone began chirping. He cracked opened the flip phone, answered the call, then switched to English. "My friend wants to know whether he should book a table tomorrow in Jockey's Club," he said to me. "What should I tell him?"

"Sounds fun," I told him. "Why not?"

The next night, I met my father's influential friend in our hotel lobby in Kowloon. He was a stubby man with a salt-and-pepper pompadour. A racing program bundled in his hand, he moved, like many people here, with a kind of impatient speed— as though, at any given moment, he was thwarted from going faster. Greeting us, he ushered us onto the street where his driver sat in an idling Mercedes sedan.

We crossed the bridge onto Hong Kong Island. I gaped again at the city's skyscrapers, which were squeezed together like the pipes of a church organ. The neon lights of the side streets bring the fizz to the soda water of the evening. The city is so unapologetically, headily urban—there's no hand-wringing here about bike lanes or preserving historic buildings—that it makes you feel more cosmopolitan, more purposeful by association. My father's efforts to ensure I enjoyed his hometown had been madly successful. In fact, often during that trip, I wondered why my parents exchanged this for a house with a backyard and children who couldn't properly speak their native language.

The driver deposited us at a side entrance alongside thousands of people streaming into the grandstands for the weekly race. My father's friend signed us in then led us to an elevator that delivered us to the Jockey's Club before leaving us at a table with copies of the program. "You'll have to excuse me," he said, as he stepped away to answer his phone. "Enjoy yourself."

From where I viewed the track, Happy Valley, first built in 1845, and then rebuilt in 1995, felt to me like a turf-covered crater in the ancient forest of high-rises. If Hastings Park comes off as a cross between a minor-league baseball stadium and an inner-city playground, Happy Valley is like a shopping mall for billionaires. Even the grandstand area, to me, resembled an apartment building, with decks of seats and luxury boxes stacked vertically. The Jockey Club itself is swishly appointed in a post-colonial manner, with dark-stained wood accents, a buffet that mixed Asian cuisine in glimmering silver steam trays, and a room half-filled with non-Chinese.

Horseracing in Hong Kong represents a confluence of the city's recent British rule and the longstanding Chinese obsession with chance. Hong Kong Chinese, in particular, seem to gamble fanatically the same way North Americans fastidiously maintain their lawns—as an act of civic pride. It's said that the Chinese are the least religious people in the world but the most superstitious, and a fixation with the vagaries of chance might be an extension of our godlessness. Or *maybe we just like to gamble.*

A waiter appeared to take our drink orders, and my father suggested I get a beer. Everything was covered, but I asked for water instead. There's a ceiling of fun that you hit with your parents, and I didn't want to knock my head against it.

I placed a few bets for myself and my mother, who would, later on that trip, spend a good hour feeding the slot machines in nearby Macau. I stepped into the balcony to watch the horses

running down the grass track: they looked like mice on Astro-
turf. An atheist in this cathedral of chance, my father refused
to place a wager. His friend would appear at our table for a few
minutes, take a bite of the roast pork tenderloin on his plate,
and then disappear to make more bets with his friends.

"What does your friend do?" I asked my dad.

"He's a property developer with quite a few factories in China.
He's been very prosperous."

According to my father, they met when he was still a bank
manager and his friend was a teenager. Every week, this kid
would come into the bank and deposit money into an account
that he would use to make a down payment on his first apartment. When it turned out that some of the money was stolen
from his own mother, my father explained to the mother that
her son wasn't doing anything bad with the money. Then he told
the boy to invest some of this money in stocks. "He's still grateful for my help," my father explained. "And now whenever I visit,
he makes sure I'm treated well."

"Is he married?" I asked. He seemed too restless that evening
to be attached to anyone.

My dad shook his head incredulously. "He's got *two* wives."

"What?"

"One is the legal wife; the other is the trophy wife—the one he
travels with."

"Do the wives know each other?" I ask.

"I hope so."

I won money on a couple of races, but, as usual, lost on balance. After a couple of hours, when I suggested we leave, my
dad, who has no stomach for betting, was happy to thank his
friend and depart.

Squeezed into a cab back to Kowloon, I recalled those photos in my grandmother's room. You hear a lot about infants who
look like a parent at one stage in their life and then resemble
the other a few months later. The assumption is that at a certain

point in late adolescence this resemblance becomes fixed. I only need to look at my father to realize it doesn't. As he's gotten older, my sixty-five-year-old father looks less like my grandfather, the man in the picture preserved in the distant past, and more like my grandmother—older and shrinking, his face kneading into itself.

I'd left my camera in my cousin's car the other night; I would have to remember this night on my own.

IT'S A LATE afternoon in May. I've been hanging around the track because I want to see the baby—the horse Randi recently bred with Sylvester's sister, who's actually named Baby (but raced under the name Hoping for Fun), in a farm outside the city. The life of Baby's baby has already been eventful. First, the little colt was born with only half of the mare's placenta out, which caused an infection that he barely survived. The foal had contracted tendons that made him walk with a mincing gait, like a ballerina on her tippy toes. The vet prescribed tetracycline, an antibiotic, to relax his tendons, but that left him knock-kneed—his legs folding in like two opposing arrow points.

Randi gathers five empty buckets. With an empty plastic coffee tin, she scoops into each bucket a can's worth of oats and sweet feed; a few teaspoons of electrolytes (the stuff found in Gatorade) and Vitamins C, K, and E, and selenium, which keeps them from tying up; some glucosamine, for their joints; a bit of "gut medicine" that comes with zinc; a few squirts of molasses from a container with a pump nozzle; and a handful of sliced-up carrots. Horses like the oft-injured Riley and a new filly, who's still recovering from an injury and not expending a lot of energy, get scoops of beet pulp to fill out their meal.

I wait for Blackie to back into her stall before I slide under the gate—I haven't figured out how to unlatch it—and dump the bucket into the feed tub in her stall.

I slip another bucket into Sylvester's stall just before the blacksmith, a tall, burly twenty-eight-year-old named Todd with short, reddish blond hair and a prematurely grizzled manner, arrives to shoe them. Afterwards, the three of us climb into Randi's car. The inside of the windshield is coated with a sticky film from a can of Coke that exploded in the car the other week.

"The baby's knees are going in and his feet are going out," Randi says, as we leave the city limits and enter the highway. "So we're shaving the outside of her legs shorter than the inside to make them try to go normal."

I wince. "Todd's going to trim his leg?"

Randi shakes her head. "You always take what I say too literally," she tells me. "Todd's going to trim his hoof. The hoof is like a toenail."

From the back seat, I lean over to Todd. "What will you be using to do that?"

Todd points to a rasper—an outsized nail file attached to a wooden handle.

We arrive at the farm in the early evening. Thoroughbreds grazing behind a fence watch us without interest. Inside a small, unattended barn, a transistor radio is playing "Wichita Lineman" by Glen Campbell. The bay-coloured, month-old foal is in a stable with Baby. He will remain with his mother until September or October, at which point he'll become a weanling. Next year, Randi will try to get a good price for him at the yearling auction; failing that, she'll attempt to run the horse in a stakes race open only to locally bred horses.

Todd steps into the stable followed by Randi. "It doesn't make no fucking sense why the fuck the vet wants it so high," he says to her, hands on hips. "It just seems like you'd want it high on the inside."

"You want me to phone her?" Randi asks.

"I'll do what the vet wants to get done," Todd says. "That way, if anything goes wrong, it's *not my fault*." He approaches the foal, who bites him. "Guess what, you fucking know better trying to bite me, you bitch."

Randi crouches down and holds the baby horse sideways around the legs as though she were clutching two paper bags full of groceries.

After his feet are rasped, we stand back and admire the foal, a cuddly guy who seems both annoyed and pleased by the attention.

An accredited psychologist with a degree from the University of Let Me Tell You What's Wrong With The World would link Randi's attachment to horses, if not also her machine-gun spew of expletives and a demeanour that's crustier than a front lawn in January, to the premature loss of her mother. This is the diagnosis that I quickly latch onto—my working hypothesis. Although she buys little presents for the kids on her mail route at Christmas, Randi's never wanted children of her own. I try to picture Randi nursing a child the way she handles a foal, and at first I figure she'd be too rough with a baby. I see her teaching her own kid to brawl as a toddler. I see her bringing up a kid who would utter, as his or her first word, a pejorative term for the female anatomy. I see a kid placing over-under odds at his peewee soccer games. I see Randi putting her own kid up for auction in the yearling sales.

But then I realize that what I can't see is Randi *wanting* to push a stroller. She would be a great parent, if she had to be. She could be source material for one of those movies, like Gena Rowlands in *Gloria* or Adam Sandler in *Big Daddy*, in which a deliberately childless person is handed custody of a toddler and learns to be a loving, if unorthodox parent. Horses, after all, are delicate in their own way.

The baby edges away when I try to pet him.

"He's got a cute little mug on him," Randi admits, before lighting a smoke and addressing the foal, whom she later names Freddy, directly. "Dude, you better not be gibbled."

AFTER DROPPING TODD off at a bus stop in New Westminster, Randi takes a winding on-ramp to the highway back to Hastings, where I'm parked and where Randi's friend and client Ardenne is awaiting her at the casino. The traffic is less gnarled on the way back. I'm happy to be up front with the window down. Even half of one of Randi's workdays exhausts me.

"Where did my smokes go?" she asks. "I might have lost them."

This is the third time today that Randi has searched frantically for her smokes. She panics about her cigarettes the way some people worry about leaving the stove on.

"You probably misplaced them," I suggest.

She finds the smokes in a pocket of her mailbag. "Okay, here they are."

Randi tells me she's been smoking since she was twelve. "I quit once for seven years, it was all right," she says, one side of her mouth dropping, looking unimpressed. "I always kind of wanted a smoke. I taught myself to knit because I couldn't stand not having something to do with my hands. I just can't sit around."

The flow of traffic congeals as we approach some roadwork.

"What was your mom like?" I ask her as the roller coaster in Playland comes into view. It's been a question I wanted to ask for a while now.

"She was like a mom, you know what I mean?"

I nod.

"She stayed home with the kids. It's weird how that can happen and affect all sorts of things. I think that's why I can't stand people who are whining all the time and can't do nothing for themselves."

Actually, the opposite is true. Randi almost completely surrounds herself with helpless creatures and people who both infuriate her and satisfy her need to be needed.

I don't say this, of course, but, this time at least, Randi seems to catch herself in a contradiction. "I mean, I might put up with you and pay for your stuff," she says, "but I'll think of you as useless."

LATER THAT WEEK, on the day of Blackie's fourth race that season, it's hard to say whether Randi's pessimism about the horse's chances is just her everyday pessimism, or whether she truly dislikes Blackie's chances against what she deems, with the exception of nine-year-old Grayross Gal, a "bunch of pigs."

Trainers are routinely pessimistic the way horseplayers are perpetually optimistic. In either case, good luck merely confirms their disposition. A down-to-his-last-penny punter who hits a big bet thinks the universe has finally righted itself. A long-suffering trainer whose horse manages to win reminds herself of all the races where the same horse has lost running better.

"The vet scoped Blackie and said she has a paralyzed flapper," Randi announces in her tack room. "That's why she lulls at the ends."

A horse has two flappers in its larynx, which are made of cartilage and regulate the air that gets into its lungs. A common affliction among horses, a paralyzed flapper restricts a horse's oxygen intake and adversely affects its performance.

"Can you do anything about it?" I ask Randi.

She shakes her head. "You can give her some bronchial dilators, but you're not allowed to run on them. She's probably only getting eighty percent of her air, on one side."

Even with this diagnosis, Randi's more worried that law of averages will work against Blackie, who has already put forth three good efforts and is due for a poor outing. "She's run hard three times already in the past six weeks," she says. "That's not easy."

I return to the frontside because I've invited my parents to the race. I made a reservation for 3:30 PM at Silks, the track restaurant, fully expecting them to be late. Tardiness runs in my bloodline, just like gout and nearsightedness. Inviting them here is something new for me. As a kid, I didn't really want my parents at my school concerts or games, lest it ruin that version of myself carefully constructed for the consumption of friends. Out of habit, this practice has extended into my adulthood. My life outside our family has always been related to them in a self-consciously offhand, casual way. In breaking out of this routine, I'm doing this to show them why I'm at the track, and also because it's Father's Day tomorrow.

When my parents arrive, I lead them to our table overlooking the finish line. We order lunch just as the horses are led through the post parade.

"Which one is yours?" my dad asks, looking out the plate-glass window.

"Number seven."

My dad, in a checked blazer and turtleneck, peruses the racing program. "Why aren't you listed as an owner?" he asks me.

"The paperwork is still being processed."

My dad sniffs. "Are you sure they didn't just take your money?"

My mother's amused that I have to own a horse in order to write about it. "I'm glad you're not writing about lion-taming," she says. "Or homosexuality."

I begin to gasp but swallow my astonishment. "Not at the moment."

My father, still suspicious of my racing involvement, scans the room, as though he's afraid he'll be mugged. "When you wrote about the ladies of the night," my dad says, referring to an article I wrote about survival sex workers for a women's magazine, "did you bring one home with you?"

I cringe and shake my head. On our trip to Macau in March, my dad wanted to take me and my mom to the place where the sex workers gathered to parade themselves in a circle. I had to beg my dad not to go. I really don't know what it is, maybe some kind of atavistic paternal yearning, but he seems to enjoy picturing me with a professional.

"The race is starting," I tell them. "She's number seven."

The horses emerge from the top of the lane. With Perez on her again, Blackie narrowly avoids a competitor bobbling out of the gate and weaves towards the rail as they head into the clubhouse turn and the jockeys flash their white breeches at us. At the first turn, Blackie is three-quarters of a length behind Grayross Gal, who's wearing white blinders.

"Twenty-three and change," I announce. "She's still got gas in her tank."

Perez keeps his lines low on Blackie, holding back the horse, whose mane is whipping back in pretty tendrils, from going at full speed. He loosens his grip at the half-mile mark, allowing the horse to make her move; he drops one hand from the reins and gives the horse a couple of swats. Rider and horse take a half-length lead over Grayross Gal at the top of the front stretch.

My mother yelps and my father bunches his hands together as Blackie builds on her lead. Blackie's knees start going higher, as though she knows her victory is already clinched. On replays, it definitely looks as though she's skipping to the finish.

Maybe the sweetest moments in life are those exhilarating seconds that precede your getting something you really, really want. Not getting what you want stinks, obviously. And getting what you want happens so infrequently it can be too dumbfounding to enjoy completely, it can lead to disappointment or some other unforeseen, ironic complications. But the time that elapses between knowing you're going to get something good and getting it is like a death march in reverse—a joy march. It's as if helium is running through your bloodstream, your head and your limbs feel like parade floats tethered to your feet. Your heart fills out your chest like a bag of microwave popcorn. Your face tingles as though you're mainlining champagne.

There are maybe ten seconds after Blackie takes the lead where her victory seems all but certain, where I can safely savour victory; it's like cheering for a team with two minutes left in the game and an insurmountable lead. If the average person were to add up those moments of bliss, would it even exceed the time it takes for him to get to work on any given day, or the time spent waiting on hold with the cable company? I doubt it.

"IT'S MOCHA TIME TO SCORE," the announcer says from the loudspeakers. "GRAYROSS GAL SECOND, MYSTIC PASS THIRD."

Not having trained or taken care of the horse, not even having been a fractional owner for more than two months, I don't really deserve to feel as proud as I do. It's not my style to act as though I care about things; I am not one to emote. But then I flash through all the times that life hasn't set up for me the way I wanted it to, all the close calls, turn-downs, coulda-beens, wish-I-hads, aches, and regrets. I turn to my parents beside me, who put up with my glowering teenage years and noisy guitar noodling, whose cars I dented, who put me through an expensive grad school, and whom I haven't repaid with grandchildren. I decide not to fight this feeling.

Even my father, who could never resist indulging my passions, no matter how foolish and expensive—I had a better guitar collection that any sixteen-year-old I knew—is swayed by my enthusiasm.

"I'm going down to the track for the winner's photo," I tell my dad. "You want to join me?"

"That's okay," he says. "Enjoy yourself."

I bounce down the stairs between owner's boxes and to the apron, where I shake hands with Randi's crew and Blackie's other owners—people I only met in passing. We step into the winner's circle, which resembles a bus stop with its glass awning, where we each, in turn, give Randi a hug and shake the jockey's hand.

"I could get used to this," I tell Randi, who's not so much excited as she is pleased that everyone around her is so happy.

Randi tells me to turn my head. "Look at the photographer."

9

SID MARTIN, PART ONE

A WEEK AFTER BLACKIE'S win, I'm still strutting as though I have a tallboy beer can for a dong—shoulders flung back, chin in the air, theoretical package up front like a blind man's cane. How soon before I need my own urethra bean extracted? When relating this victory, I begin by saying how richly undeserved it is, but then proceed to explain, with my eyes flashing like safety flares, how I had it coming to me.

Even while seated at my desk, I can barely lock down this cocky swing. It's past midnight when I drop my work—online research in preparation for an assignment in the Yukon—to begin writing my how-to manual on leadership and success: *The Winning Ticket Inside You*. The cover would have me in a leather jacket, holding a glass of champagne while sitting atop Blackie. My fingers prance along the keyboard at full speed:

CHAPTER ONE

Don't let your miserable bank balance fool you: it's not how much you invest, but how much you invest of *yourself.*

All my life the pulsing desire to become a professional sports owner persisted, if not in the foreground, then in the bowels of my hopes and aspirations. Not being even faintly interested in the nicknaming and group showering that denotes jock culture, I nonetheless loved competition, the talent portion of the pissing contest—when you go for accuracy, flair, and eye contact. I wanted to live, like the gamer at his frosting-smudged keyboard gaping at his onscreen avatar, through the exertions of finely trained athletes, whose physical cunning and hard-won skills were catalyzed by their unstinting impulse to outrace, evade, and topple their opponents, to share in their triumphs and the crushing disappointments that set up the victories sweeter than grape drink and barbecue sauce.

As I survey my Tudor-style estate with garden topiary in the shapes of arrowheads and sea cucumbers, my library filled with first editions of other bestselling manuals and literary erotica, my closet stuffed with never-worn socks, and as my super-stacked wife—a physics professor and former elbow model—brings me pancakes in bed after delivering our three beloved children to boarding school for their fall term, I recall how it all started when I bought a cheap thoroughbred named Mocha Time.

She was the horse no one believed in; I was the part owner who needed to learn how to believe in himself...

Of course, the scenario I present is fully delusional—at least for now. To make myself credible, I need triumphs that will lead to adversities that will make me hungry and grateful for the crowning triumph. To that end, I decide to buy into another racehorse.

The next day, while we're on her mail route, I tell Randi about my plan. We're now midway into the racing season and the weather has turned muggy. I hold together in the heat as well as a chocolate bar, so, to avoid turning into a sweet, brown puddle, I hide under trees while Randi slips through the squawky metal gates of another house.

"At the rate Blackie's going," I tell Randi, early on the route, when I'm still chatty, "I'm going to break even—at least. So, I figure, why not double down?"

"Well, there's no guarantee she'll break even. You'd be lucky if that happens."

"I know, I know."

"The only horse I have is Sylvester. Unless you want to buy into Riley."

"Well, I was thinking of maybe getting another trainer."

"Oh," she says, breaking into a smile. "Why not?"

"It might be fun to meet other people at the track. And also, I want to diversify my holdings."

"Yeah, I figured you for somebody who won't go all in on one thing," she says. "You kind of float around, don't you?"

"Yeah..." Why did I think it was a secret?

It doesn't take long for the heat to wear us both down. Saddled with a bag of mail on each of her hips, Randi starts staggering, her elbows pinned to her sides. (Canada Post forbids non-employees from handling the mail, so I can't help carry her bags.) Clutching mail to her chest, she approaches each door as though she were a mime pulling an imaginary plough. At one house, she finds a garden hose and douses her head; she seems no less relieved than the horses she waters down after a gallop. She perks up momentarily when the dogs on her route run up to their backyard gates and start yapping deliriously. To the animals that don't cost her money, she's the fun aunt, throwing three or four biscuits apiece.

"You know what I need?" she asks me after tossing out Milk-Bones. "I need my own cookie. The other day, someone gave me a cookie because I looked like I was going to fucking die. She said, 'Oh, you look so awful, I brought you a cookie.' Well, I said, 'Fuck, I was going to kill myself, you saved my life.'"

"Was it a good cookie?" I ask her.

"Oh, it was fucking awesome," she says, laughing. "It had chocolate chips, pecan, and cranberry. And it was freshly baked."

Randi's got a registered letter for this woman today, so if she's home, she's going to ask her for more cookies.

"I ain't shy that way," she adds.

"Get on it, then."

By the time we reach Adanac, a street with almost no shade, I can't be bothered to speak much. As she pulls out the registered mail, Randi turns to me: "This is the lady who gave me cookies." I watch from the sidewalk as an elderly woman with glasses and a perm answers the door. She doesn't recognize Randi.

Randi presents the registered mail for her to sign. "The other day, your daughter gave me a cookie."

"Yes?" the woman says, with an accent that I can't quite locate. She signs the package.

"They were really good cookies. You don't have any left over, do you?"

"Yes," she says flatly, placing one hand on the edge of the door.

At this point, I could go for a midday sugar boost myself, but this woman takes the registered mail from Randi and shuts the door without even thanking her.

This snub makes Randi extra-generous with the next dog that comes mooching for a snack. Once she's completed her route, we get into her car and get iced coffee from a Starbucks drive thru, only a few blocks from Hastings.

"If you really want to buy another horse, you don't want one of them new-age guys," Randi says between sips. "You need to find someone old school, someone who remembers how great racing used to be."

"Who'd you suggest?" I ask.

She thinks, then her eyes pop. "What about Sid Martin?"

"Who's he?"

"Sid's from the old days. He was a jockey here, long time ago in the forties," she says, as we turn onto Renfrew Street. "Then he became a big-shot trainer in California. I worked for him at Santa Anita in the seventies, but he only remembers me from when he came back here, about twenty years ago. Do you know he had a horse that finished third in the Kentucky Derby in the seventies?"

"*Wow.*"

"The same horse finished third in the Preakness and fourth at Belmont."

"When's he at the track?" I ask.

"In the morning, like everyone else. We could look for him tomorrow."

"Actually," I say, "I'll be in Dawson City for an assignment."

"You're always going places, aren't you?"

It's true. I'm always hot for an excuse to board a plane, especially when there's someone else footing the bill. Unlike Randi, I don't mind "visiting"—seeing the sights and drinking local beer—so long as I can leave before getting bored.

But when you're coming and leaving, again and again, it starts feeling as if you're not arriving anyplace new. You're going the same direction, around and around. Then again, maybe everything reminds me of horseracing these days.

I MEET WITH Sid Martin when I get back to town. At eighty, he is trim and precise in his appearance. His blue eyes seem granite-carved in a circumspect squint, and he keeps his top lip in a flat line, like a big-league coach who's accustomed to scrutiny from the cheap seats. Slightly built, he has a neatly tapered face, with a swoop of wavy white hair underneath his tweed flat cap. I find him outside Barn M and he leads me to his car. In a cardboard box, he has four thick albums' worth of material.

"That has everything you'll need to know. If it was this day and age, you'd never have these scrapbooks," Martin says, cracking open one album. "The newspapers don't cover it anymore."

By the opened rear door of his station wagon, we begin flipping through the carefully preserved collection of newspaper clippings, photos, letters, telegrams, get-well cards, and old racing programs. When I find out that Sid currently trains four horses, three of which he owns, I mention my desire to buy into another horse. "Would you be willing to sell a share of one of your horses?" I ask.

"Two of them are sick with this cough going around the track," he says, brushing off my assistance and carrying the heavy box into the trunk of my car.

"I understand that a horse at the track died," I say.

He nods. "I wouldn't be doing you any favours."

Martin—who was born in 1929, the ninth of ten children, in New Brunswick, before moving to Vancouver at the age of four—suggests we sit down at Trackers for lunch. As he recounts his racing glories, he speaks in a low mumble that comes from his disciplinarian father, an upholsterer who served in the British Navy at fourteen. "I wouldn't dare say 'Speak up' to him," Martin says. "I talk as low as I do because of him."

In his whispery voice, Martin explains how his entry into racing came through one of his brothers, who shared a tent in the army reserves with a prominent local bookmaker, Abe Forshaw, during World War II. Martin's brother told Forshaw about his runty younger brother, who was fourteen and weighed only seventy-five pounds, and the bookie gave Sid's brother a note to hand to his trainer Sleepy Armstrong, who ushered eventual Hall of Fame jockey Johnny Longden to riding. Sid started out as a hot walker and groom, making five bucks a week.

Martin only made it to Grade 8, passing off his aversion to book-learning as a family trait. "I told people I was in Grade 4 four times," he jokes, "because they didn't want me in the same room as my dad."

In re-telling his stories, Martin steadies his voice as he builds to his punchlines. The squinty blue eyes flash momentarily behind his square-ish, wire-frame glasses and when he laughs the tension drains from his face, which ripples as he smiles. You expect to hear an imaginary rim shot and cymbal crash after one of his better zingers—like that joke about his dad being a superannuated fourth-grade student, which I later find in a newspaper article published four decades earlier.

Under trainer George Irvine, Martin galloped in Vancouver, Winnipeg, and New York, where he remembers watching Triple Crown winner Assault and fellow champion Stymie "kick the hell out of each other" in training. It was at Jamaica in New York that Martin got his jockey's licence, though he received his first mount as an apprentice rider, or "bug boy," in Seattle in 1947. At Longacres, he broke his maiden on his fourth mount on one of Irvine's horses, Latin Agent. (Like "backside," the term "maiden" has a couple of meanings in racing parlance. It's used to describe horses, male and female, that have never won a race. A new jockey can also "break" his or her maiden with his first victory.)

"Martin went to work with a vengeance and poured through the stretch to a lip victory in a three-way photo," reads one unattributed newspaper clipping in his scrapbook. "A live boy and apparent[ly] fearless, the curly-headed youngster seems destined for a chunk of fame on horseback." One day that year, Martin would win on every one of his mounts, going five for five. "Don't ask me how it happened," the teenaged Martin says in another clipping. "We just seemed to get there first—all five of us." (He must have meant "all six of us"—or was misquoted.)

That season, he was the leading apprentice and second overall rider at Longacres, and the leading rider at Playfair in Spokane.

Martin was a jockey for another year, racing at Lansdowne, the other track in Vancouver's suburbs, as well as Bay Meadows in California and Caliente in Mexico. In his third season, Martin—on the tall end for his profession and therefore prone to weight issues—found himself fighting horizontal expansion.

"Did you flip?" I ask Martin, using the innocuous-sounding jockey term for the habit of self-induced vomiting that helps desperate riders make weight. Flipping can leave riders malnourished and weak, and has been cited as a cause of rider fatalities.

Martin, who now weighs 138 pounds, says he dabbled briefly with flipping, "but there were riders who were riding thirty years and they did that every day."

From those jockey days, Martin recalls extreme diets—one in which he ate only tomatoes and eggs—and running in a rubber suit to keep his weight under 115 pounds. After his second season, he decided not to ride, and let his weight climb to 152 pounds. "They talked me into trying to ride the third year," Martin remembers. "I couldn't have an ounce of fat or liquid and the most I could get down to was 117 stripped—that means 122. The day before the races started, I quit. I ordered a steak and, while I was eating that steak, I ordered another one and, within three days, I was back to 150 pounds."

For five years after he was finished as a rider, he hung around the track as a jockey's room attendant and an exercise rider and worked at a men's clothing store before he picked up his trainer's licence in 1954 and won big races at Hastings, including a one-two finish in the 1965 B.C. Premier's Championship with Costa Rica and Fleet Runner. (One of the horses Martin currently owns is named T Drive, the name of a local stakes winner he had in the 1950s. With the exception of famous horses—you can't, for instance, name your colt

Seabiscuit—a thoroughbred's name can be recycled five years after the original horse finishes racing.)

In 1967, Colin Campbell, a local businessman who'd made his fortune building highways during the war, offered Martin a job as a private trainer for his horses at Santa Anita and Hollywood Park. Martin was thirty-seven, married with a young family, and well established at Hastings when he accepted that job. "I didn't want to spend my life thinking 'I could've been big league,'" he says.

At this point in retelling his life story, Martin finishes his tuna fish sandwich, taps the pack of cigarettes in his shirt pocket, and asks me if I'd mind sitting outside. We settle in a seat on the patio, where Martin resumes his story while chain-smoking. After winning races like the Argonaut Stakes and the Milady Handicap, Martin began training for others, including another Canadian high roller, oilman Frank McMahon, who won the Kentucky Derby and Preakness with Majestic Prince in 1969. "He was a delightful man to work for," Martin says through a veil of smoke. "I'd just explain what I was doing and he wouldn't interfere. He was a gem because his word was so good."

In 1973, McMahon spent $47,000 on a dark bay colt sired by Damascus, who won the Preakness and Belmont in 1967, from a mare called Bill And I, "who was the queen of the bushes in Ohio." The horse's vowel-heavy name, Diabolo, was the result of a clerical error that added an extra "o." Working the colt at Hollywood Park with three other colts McMahon had just bought in Kentucky, Martin knew he had a special horse from the start. "He went down in twenty-two and three," he remembers. "Ninety percent of horses can't run that fast in the afternoon. He pulls up in thirty-four"—over three furlongs—"and the clocker said, 'Who *in the hell* was that?'"

With racing legend Willie Shoemaker aboard, Diabolo won the Del Mar Futurity as a two-year-old. Laffit Pincay, Jr., who eventually broke Shoemaker's record of career wins, took over as rider the next year in 1975 at the California Derby, where the colt broke Noor and Citation's jointly held track record for nine furlongs at Golden Gate Fields. This led to Martin's one trip to the Triple Crown.

"It was nice to know there was a runner in the barn," Martin says, smiling. Of the thousands of horses he's trained, this will be the one he'll always remember first.

IT'S PAST MIDNIGHT and, as normal, I'm bolted to my lap-top. A problematic passage in a story leads to Internet research, which leads to Internet dawdling, before finally, inevitably, end-ing with Internet creeping. For the past hour, I've been sifting through the online leavings of Linda Lee, who's gone from being "In a Relationship" to conspicuously un-listing her status on her online profile.

Eventually, cyber-stalker's remorse kicks in and I cautiously back away from my computer as though it were a bear on hind legs. On my kitchen table, basically an open-faced storage unit, Sid Martin's box of scrapbooks sits without yet being parsed. I pluck a Stella Artois from the fridge and lug the first book to my armchair.

The material starts from the beginning of his racing career, when he was only a teenager: the photos of him galloping a horse; the shots of him as a jockey in the winner's circle with women in hats, finger-wave hairdos, and fur coats; the news-paper clipping of his first win at Longacres in Seattle. Martin's scrapbooks are like the photo-lined walls in Randi's break room.

It makes sense for an eighty-year-old man to have such doc-umentation of his accomplishments, but then my imagination creaks trying to imagine the teenager who first put these clip-pings together. Most young adults I know have enough trouble remembering where they left their cell phones. Certainly, Sid had to have been a meticulous young man, or maybe his mother started cutting out the newspaper articles. It occurs to me that this isn't the scrapbook of a teenager who felt he was destined for greatness so much as it's the collection of a young man who realized, right from the start, that he was part of a world that contained greatness, excitement, and glamour.

When I finish my beer, I pick up the next scrapbook while looping back from the fridge. This binder covers Sid Martin's Triple Crown year, when Diabolo came tantalizingly close to victory in all three races. It's the Kentucky Derby, in particular, that gets Martin most excited, or, at least, it takes up the most scrapbook space.

Martin includes a long letter that his wife Grace photocopied and sent to her friends right after returning from Louisville. With no feigned worldliness, Mrs. Martin's letter captures the excitement of being a VIP at the Run for the Roses: the first-class plane ride, the banquets held in honour of the trainers, the TV and radio interviews, and luminaries like Ferdinand and Imelda Marcos, the "Six Million Dollar Man," and Howard Cosell. The Martins sat in a box near the finish line with Frank McMahon and his family. "The governor called 'hello' to Sid from his box behind us," wrote Grace Martin, who passed away from cancer at fifty-four. (Martin's current partner, Dawn, works at one of the mutuel windows at Hastings.) "Glen Campbell and his wife were with him. I thought Glen gave me [a] sexy little wink, but maybe he had dust in his eye. I'll never know!!"

Diabolo, a fidgety horse who used to thwack a tetherball outside of his stall to keep himself occupied, was calm in the days before they left for Louisville on a chartered plane. Martin, in contrast, was "sleeping only 2 or 3 hours a night and couldn't seem to keep his meals down ... the horse arrived in grand condition," writes Grace, who had her husband's knack for zingers, "but the vets gave Sid a tranquilizer."

I edge back to my computer and enter "Kentucky Derby 1975" into YouTube. A two-minute clip pops up. The twenty horses emerge from the gate—a burst dam of coursing horseflesh.

Hanging outside, Diabolo, in yellow blinkers, moves up from the back half of the field to sixth in the backstretch. The infield spectators at Churchill Downs rush the rail as the horses pass them; many of the people bounce in the air, hoping for a better view. "He weaves himself through, horse after horse, like drawing a map," Martin told me earlier. "He got where you want to be at the quarter pole. And then he went after Avatar."

At the far turn, Diabolo is on the outside duking it out with Avatar, another California horse ridden by Shoemaker, for the lead. The race is going perfectly for Martin and his horse. As Diabolo and Avatar change leads—when horses turn, the leg that leads out must be inside—they bump into each other. Diabolo gets the worst of the collision and loses his stride going down the lane. Foolish Pleasure, the race favourite, dances ahead of both horses to reach the wire first, followed by Avatar, who'd later win the Belmont. Diabolo recovers, eventually, to finish two lengths behind in third.

"First Diabolo bobbled, and then, recovering, lugged in on Avatar," Whitney Tower wrote in the *Sports Illustrated* cover story of the race. "Almost as if in self-defense Avatar bumped Diabolo, knocking him completely off stride and just as completely out of contention."

When we spoke, Martin clearly disagreed with the assertion, but wouldn't elaborate. "Anything you say will sound like sour grapes," he told me. "Those things are what you call history."

Watching this race, though, inspires me to fire up my word processor and begin another section of *The Winning Ticket Inside You.*

CHAPTER TWO

We have all had failures in life. The early setbacks in my life were nothing special: manuscripts bounced, articles quashed, and futile personal prospects that I pursued down online cul-de-sacs. What compounded these losses—the real failure—was my inability to get past them.

The eventual victors quickly forget the hurt, even if it kills them. One good strategy is to employ humour. At the track, I learned this lesson from a venerable horseman who had come as close as possible to winning his profession's greatest baubles, only to have them cruelly wrenched away from him by ill fortune. "I've always been able to look at the funny side," he told me, three decades after his near-triumph. "There's no use crying because it only gets your cheeks wet." So many years after his disappointments, he still laughs, even if the smile is rubbery and stiff on his face, like a dental dam...

⇒ 10 ⇐

LEARN ANOTHER LANGUAGE

AN INTERMINABLE MONTH, the plumpest patch of summer, passes between races for my horse. During this once-a-year spasm of uninterrupted sunshine in Vancouver, it's as if every man, woman, and child in the city has come upon a $20 bill on the street. The people I know scramble around manically, making weekend plans on island cabins or campgrounds; work becomes an obligation that's discharged half-consciously, the way you load your dishwasher.

Still wired from the horse's success, I want to while away this intoxication in public, where I feel my magic will have the greatest effect. Of course, the horse figures in all my social interactions, my trump card to end conversational threads involving child-rearing and yoga classes. The only hitch for me is that when I tell people I'm a part owner of a racehorse, it automatically prompts them to wisecrack, "Which part of the horse?"

After hearing that joke about six hundred times, I attempt to alter the wording. I say I am a fractional owner, a co-owner, a shareholder of a racehorse. But people still ask me *which part of the horse I own.* Eventually, I turn the joke around by saying I'm only *part of an owner.*

"Which part?" I'm then asked.

"I'll give you a hint," I say, holding up the back of my hand. "It's one of these fingers."

In June, I find myself at the wedding reception of a high-school friend in the ballroom of a harbourfront hotel. I'm seated with a couple I've met only twice before—the others at the table are strangers. After a prolonged debate about the wisdom of measles vaccinations for children, I allow myself to expound on Blackie. This, naturally, leads to a brief overview of horse masturbation techniques.

"Colts please themselves by thrusting their erect dinks in the air or bouncing them against their stomachs," I say, flapping and jabbing my forearm to simulate both kinds of masturbation. The guys' eyes gleam like polished silverware; their companions' carry expressions of dismay.

"So would a horse breeder want to eliminate this as a way of preserving the stud's *juices?*" one guy, a cousin of the bride, asks me; his wife hands him the stink-eye. "Or would the horse have enough to go around?"

I scratch my chin—only because it's itchy. "According to my information, a horse doesn't usually ejaculate when he masturbates," I say. "But I also read a *scholarly* article that says that breeders will discourage stallions from masturbating through 'schemes and devices such as stallion rings, brushes, and cages.'"

(In that same article, entitled "Spontaneous Erection and Masturbation in Equids," its author, Sue M. McDonnell, also observes that "when the horse was bouncing or thrusting the penis, the facial expression usually suggested pleasure and contentment similar to the kind observed during solitary grooming. A trance-like, glazed-eye appearance was occasionally evident.")

There's one woman at the table who's been brought to the wedding by her boyfriend. Earlier in the evening, our conversation about books halted shortly after she told me she only read titles about gender theory and spirituality. She works in information services at one of the local universities, has high cheekbones, frizzy black hair, and wears a nose stud.

"Let me say I'm sure this project of yours is well-meaning," she tells me, leaning across the table. "So you might not be aware of how *disgusting* horseracing really is."

"Is it because of the bean?" I ask, nodding at the dried-out piece of horse smegma lying in front of my salmon dinner.

She ignores the bean. "I'm sure you're doing this with good intentions, but I don't think you understand the cruelty of horseracing."

"Have you ever even been to a racetrack?" I ask her, trying not to sound peeved as I pocket the bean again.

"I go riding horses every other weekend," she says. "The cruelty of horseracing is well-known."

"But have you ever been to a racetrack?" I ask again.

She deflects this question as though I'm trying to trick her into the back of my idling van. The tone of voice she adopts isn't argumentative, but lulling, like an adult trying to talk a child out of an irrational fear. "At the track, horses die every day from broken legs and bleeding lungs. Do you know that?"

Her boyfriend looks away, sawing through his chicken breast intently.

"But that's only a fraction of the races," I say limply. In fact, it's four in every thousand races in North America—and the ratio continues dropping.

"And every day, horses, which are natural pack animals, live in confined spaces."

"Dogs and cats are pack animals, too," someone at the table suggests, "but no one thinks it's cruel when people adopt them."

"Horses get used to being in stalls," I add.

Right then, someone at the head table starts clinking his wineglass, and the attention of the room shifts. The Woman

Who Hates Horseracing waits until the bride and groom smooch. "They don't get used to it," she announces into the applause that accompanies the matrimonial osculation. "Their spirits are broken."

NOWADAYS, GOING TO the track when my horse isn't racing is like being a parent at a kids' soccer game that doesn't involve his own child. Okay, it's less disturbing than that, but you know what I mean—it's not as fun. And yet, in the long stretch between contests for Blackie, I can't stay away from Hastings. The gambling bug has fixed onto me and has exploded from too much blood.

Visiting the track prompts me to ask myself continually how to proceed when you love doing something you'll never be good at doing. Normally, with newfound passions that require talent and practice, either I dabble and lose interest (e.g., with darts and bowling) or I go full-tilt and lose perspective (e.g., with online Scrabble). I'm starting to realize I'll never be a successful horseplayer—I'm both too cautious and too indifferent. Whatever I bet I can afford to lose, but I don't want to make wild, uninformed wagers, either. As well, when I open the *Form*, I start copy editing for style and grammar.

This last realization proves inspiring one Sunday afternoon. Maybe what I need to do, if I can't win money, is to meld the sport with my own actual talents. As a word nerd, I should instead master racing's idioms and slang, an achievable goal that also serves another non-essential purpose. I remove my to-do list from the wall above my computer and strike a line through one of my items:

1. ~~BECOME A HOME OWNER~~ BOUGHT A RACEHORSE
2. ~~FIND TRUE LOVE~~ VISITED A BREEDING SHED
3. SETTLE DOWN & START A FAMILY
4. SEE THE WORLD

5. ~~LEARN ANOTHER LANGUAGE~~ TALKED LIKE A RAILBIRD
6. ~~START A RETIREMENT PLAN~~ REDUCED GAMBLING
   LOSSES
7. GET A TATTOO

I've already learned from Randi that a horse that "pukes" in a race quit in it—and didn't actually hurl; that an apprentice rider is called a "bug boy" because the asterisk beside his name on the program is insect-like; the favourite in a race is called "the chalk" from the days when odds were tallied, and erased, on a blackboard; a "rabbit" is a horse that runs up front early in the race, setting the pace before finishing well behind it; and that "Upset" is the name of the only horse who beat Man o' War. (It's been erroneously claimed that the meaning of the word "upset" as an underdog victory originated from this 1919 race.) While I know I'll never pass for a horseman, at least I can use their lingo properly.

Aside from an occasional copy error, the *Form* is another joyous source of esoteric language. It has race information found in the program, like previous race results, Beyer Speed Figures (designed by *Washington Post* columnist and star handicapper Andrew Beyer to account for differences in distance and track surface to provide a standardized rating of a horse's speed), and trainer winning percentages, but it also contains an excess of commentary. Riffling through my copy one summer Sunday, I can't help thinking that the racetrack could use some of the PR spin and the coddling euphemisms of constructive criticism seen in every other corner of public discourse.

I mean, in what other context would "failing to menace" be such a bad thing? Boxing, I guess. But in most other places, failing to menace would be regarded more positively, and in other occupations, children's entertainment or restaurant hostessing, say, it would be grounds for a positive workplace evaluation. How about instead of *failed to menace,* maybe *made everyone feel at home?* Similarly, a horse that *set pace, gave way* should be described as *didn't need to prove anything, okay with himself.* Why beat up on a horse that already lost?

But in fact, I'm here this Sunday not for the reading material, but to meet with Chad Hoverson, the most veteran rider at Hastings. After I befriended him in the cafeteria, Hoverson invited me into the jocks' room, where the riders dress and mill about. I've told him that I'm hoping to land a magazine assignment about the subject—a few years ago, I sold an article about the grooms imported from Mexico to deal with a labour shortage—but in truth, I just need a pretext for a peek-a-boo.

The space is lined with stalls for the riders. The veteran riders have marked their areas with engraved nameplates; other, friskier jockeys have covered their stalls with topless girlie photos. Near the front of the room the riders are weighed by the enchantingly named Clerk of Scales. Valets hurry around with riding equipment and towels. The track simulcast plays on a screen in the middle of the room.

As I sit with Hoverson, the jocks' room disappoints me with its camaraderie and locker-room ball-breaking—I was, in fact, hoping for more friction. The fifty-five-year-old assures me it's only jolly before the races begin.

"There was a fight the other day. One of the riders was mad at another one and the screaming got into fighting," Hoverson explains patiently in Idaho-bred American English. "It isn't like we all have our own private rooms. Stuff happens out there where things don't go right, you know, whether it's a guy who shuts you off, and the heat of the moment will get to you."

I find it hard to imagine Hoverson, who has blue eyes and thick, sandy-brown hair, in a jock-room brawl, not because he doesn't seem tough—the previous week I saw him with a black eye after he was thrown from a horse who clipped heels with an opponent—but because the veteran is probably the most courtly man I've met at Hastings. His unflappable good manners stand in contrast to the informal, off-colour worldviews found in the backstretch and belie the stereotype of jockeys as the Shetland pony–sized rock stars of the track.

Some jocks, of course, would argue they've earned their egos. After all, they ride hunched over their thousand-pound horses, their asses in the air, perpendicular to their feet. To approximate that position at home, try wrapping a bungee cord around a pole and then holding on to it while you lower yourself to a ninety-degree sitting position. And then place that pole on the bed of a truck going thirty-five miles an hour on a curving, bumpy road while someone throws mud in your eyes. Then ride a mechanical bull in a telephone booth to simulate the pain of being thrown by a horse coming out of the starting gate. I've been trail-riding twice and am sore just *sitting* on a horse as she *walks*.

Compared with grooms and hot walkers, the top jockeys are certainly paid like stars. Minus the quarter he gives to his agent, a jockey makes $50 per mount and ten percent of the purse. In 2008, for instance, Mario Gutierrez, then twenty-two, was the top rider at Hastings with $1,580,274 in winnings on 427 starts. Even at this small-time track, the top riders do pretty well for six months' work, with some of them also finding spots at winter tracks. By contrast, a less-established rider or an apprentice, someone who hasn't quite learned how to control the power of the horse and intuitively sense the pace of the race, might have to supplement his living as a gallop boy.

Hoverson, who's worked in over two dozen tracks including Santa Anita and Churchill Downs, arrived at the track at 5:30 AM to work horses, which helps him gain a sense of a thoroughbred's tendencies and preferences. His first ride is a colt—a maiden who "failed to menace" in his two trips to the gate this season—in a six-and-a-half-furlong spring for $25,000 claimers. At 10-to-1, the horse was given the second-longest preliminary odds by the morning line handicapper. "If I get lucky, I hope to lay about third in the race," he says, sitting on the bench in his stall. "He can run a bit but he's still a little green and hasn't quite figured the game out yet. I try to give him a clean trip and teach him things. You can only do what they'll let you."

Hoverson slips on the blue-and-white silks that belong to the owner of the horse. "The average rider has maybe a ten percent effect on the performance of the horse," he says. "You've got to feel what horses are capable of, what they're happy with. You've got to place your hands where they like it. Some horses like a shorter cross, some like a longer, leaner cross. Some of them don't want much of a hold; some do."

A buzzer sounds inside the jocks' room—fifteen minutes until the race—and the jockeys move into the paddock, where they make anxious banter with trainers and owners and mount their horses for the post parade. From the grandstand, I watch the race go how Hoverson doesn't want it to go. Rather than lying third, his young horse trails immediately after departing the gate, lingering on the outside from the first turn and hanging back throughout the race.

I wander back into the jocks' room after the race. "The horse is just being timid," he tells me, mopping the mud beard caked on the bottom half of his face with a sponge. "He's got more than that, but when a horse moves beside him you can feel him twitch. Instead of running like he can, running free, he's running with me pushing him, and at this point in time I can't make him go quickly as I could in the past."

Hoverson, while still the track's sixth-leading rider, is ever mindful that he's in his professional homestretch. Last year at Hastings was supposed to be the final meet for the jock, who had attended steward school in anticipation of an office job in the racing world, but the rough economy pushed him back into the saddle. In the past he would pick up eight or nine mounts in a day; now he takes only five or six to preserve his body. I ask him whether he'll miss racing.

"I'll struggle with it, but I can't do this forever," he tells me. "To be around these guys, it's my life."

At this moment, as though to give lie to his homily, another jockey named Dave Wilson strolls by to sass him: "There's a muck sack if I've ever seen one."

Later on, after heading outside and losing more money, I get a chance to speak with this piss-taking rider before the eighth race. Wilson, who was on the winner for the seventh race, is forty-one and has closely shaven hair, light blue eyes, a pinkish, newborn's complexion, and a buoyant grin. He's been the top rider at Hastings twice and last year won the B.C. Derby, the biggest race of the meet, on a horse that Hoverson had passed on. Yesterday, Wilson rode in all nine races. Today, he's practically a part-timer with six.

A seventeen-year veteran of racing, Wilson was a truck driver and already a young father—"I was young, dumb, and full of come"—when he first entered racing. "I wanted to take an air brakes course to upgrade my licence and the guy that was running the course owned a horse with a trainer. He said, 'Why do you want to drive a truck? You won't make no money.' So he brought me here. I'd only been on a horse once, but I had the right size and the right temperament: I liked going fast."

This temperament must also include a taste for pain. Wilson has broken a leg, pulled all the muscles on his ankles, and has been in fights—most recently, this season. "It was over stupid stuff about bumping into somebody, cutting somebody off," he tells me. "It happened two or three times. We were just beaking at each other for two or three weeks, then we just happened to go."

"Who won?" I ask, a smile crawling across my face as I imagine two little guys fighting—a windmill blur of wiry muscle, fluorescent fabric, and competitive spite.

Wilson grins. "I'd call it a draw. He may have had the upper hand a bit."

As we talk, Keveh Nicholls, a twenty-three-year-old rider from Barbados who was on Blackie for her first race of the season, yells something at Wilson. I can't make sense of what he's saying over the chattering of other riders; to my disappointment as a voyeur, they don't seem to be fighting words.

"He's talking to the younger kind of crowd," beaks Wilson, who's a decade younger than Hoverson.

"Story-telling Dave," says Nicholls, who's on the tall side for a jockey, has a set of short dread locks on his head, and is wearing yellow and green silks. "Ask him what happened after the first jump," he says to me, his eyes dancing merrily. "Why was he in my spot?"

I turn to Wilson with a goading, *are-you-seriously-going-to-take-that-crap-from-him?* expression, but he's smiling:

"It was a good spot to be in."

TWO DAYS AFTER our conversation at the wedding, the Woman Who Hates Horseracing sends me an email with a video link. "It might help you understand the issue from a more open-minded perspective," she writes, "if you saw this."

The video is entitled "Horse Racing: Cruelty Behind the Glamour" and set to sober, urgent piano music. Still images of horses falling face down into tracks or crashing over jumps in steeplechase events as gruesome details flash on title cards: "As pets or in the wild, horses run short distances at high speeds. For races, they are drugged, beaten and given intense training. They are expected to run a mile in under 2 minutes."

This isn't the first video I've seen like this. Horsemen will say that the bad stuff is rare and far outweighed by the positives. I'm inclined to agree, but still wish the bad stuff weren't so terrifying. Even ardent racing enthusiasts shudder at the memory of high-profile thoroughbreds like 2006 Derby winner Barbaro and 2008 Derby runner-up Eight Belles breaking down on the track, or of other, less celebrated horses being euthanized in hastily erected tents on the oval. A close-up photo of Barbaro's leg snapping while leaving the gate at the Preakness is memorably horrific.

Economics and the larceny of some horsemen also figure into the anti-racing argument. The 1986 Kentucky Derby and 1987 Breeders' Cup Classic winner Ferdinand was sent to slaughter in 2002 by his owners in Japan when his stud fees were no longer paying for his upkeep. Seventies champion Alydar, a successful studhorse, was murdered to collect a $20 million insurance payout in 1990.

That said, the trouble with this kind of video is how facts and statistics are used, without proper context, in the service of an eight-year-old's worldview. You could make a similar video, with equally gut-twisting images and misleading factoids, about dogs biting children and construct an emotionally persuasive case against dog ownership. You could screen images of unhappy kids and list a string of appalling statistics about child abuse to argue against human reproduction. These are only slightly more exaggerated examples of this onscreen rhetoric.

I doubt anyone who made this video has seen the kindness and devotion lavished on thoroughbreds I've witnessed firsthand. So I take exception with the video's suggestion that the only solution to eliminating racing fatalities is by banning the sport—with its tradition, culture, and economy—altogether. It's worth arguing that there aren't enough safeguards in the sport, but the racing industry has taken measures to enhance the welfare of the animals: reportedly safer artificial racing surfaces are required in California and a padded "Smurf" whip is employed at Woodbine in Toronto.

Another argument horsemen make is that thoroughbreds actually *want* to race; those who don't are quickly sent away from the track and turned into riding horses. In some ways, thoroughbreds are like the jockeys themselves: both destined to be in the sport by the circumstances of their birth (i.e., the stature of the jockeys, the lineage of the horses), but also by their temperaments. A true racehorse lives for the daily stimulation of training and the excitement that only comes from racing; if some breeds of horses are like Labrador retrievers, the thoroughbred is the equine equivalent of a border collie—an animal that's flummoxed and thwarted by the idea of sitting around, doing nothing.

This is the line of reasoning Randi uses. Obviously I am no expert on horses, but I'm certain the horses in Randi's stable aren't miserable. Even the mere suggestion that she somehow partakes in the cruelty of animals is personally offensive.

"I remember being a kid and finding out about the seal hunt and being so upset I wrote a letter to a government official," Randi says when I tell her about the Woman Who Hates Horseracing. "I still have it somewhere. It's so funny. I mean, life sucks—deal with it."

In the stables at the track, floor fans are blasting in front of each stall, whipping back the manes and forelocks of Randi's horses and making them seem as though they're stars in a video for an eighties hair band like Cinderella or Mr. Big.

"You could die crossing the street," Randi adds. "At least they're not bored here. The worst life for a horse is being rented out for everyone to ride. Those fuckers hate that shit."

"You mean, for birthday parties and shit?" I ask.

"You know, when you put on a bunch of people who don't know what the fuck they're doing, they're fucking miserable," she says. "They can't wait to be finished. It's just the same as having a job."

It's not hard to see why Randi would consider boredom the utmost act of cruelty.

"It's like getting a racehorse to deliver the mail," I say.

Randi laughs. "I like that."

SOMETIME AFTER THIS conversation, I find myself assigned to write a magazine story about the killing of wild horses in the foothills of Sundre, Alberta. It's a story I pitch partly because of my experiences at the track.

After flying into Calgary, I travel an hour and a half north to Sundre to meet the founders of the Wild Horses of Alberta Society, Doreen and Bob Henderson. Bob, a retired twenty-six-year veteran of the Calgary police, has blue-grey eyes that draw in when he smiles; Doreen has dark hair with highlights splashed across her bangs and a pinhead-sized nose stud. As Bob drives out of Sundre proper, the hills in the distance are covered with dirty-blond grass with patches of snow like dandruff.

For the Hendersons, a shared passion for horses is the linchpin to their marriage. "We came from different persuasions," Bob tells me from behind the wheel. "I have a police background and am a country cowboy. She was a city girl—a headbanger, a rock 'n' roll queen."

Doreen learned to ride as a child. "I got away from horses until I met Bob," she explains. "Then I bought my own and we started our life together. We're both horse-crazy."

The Hendersons fell in love with the wild horses on their long rides through these hills and have two rescued "wildies" on their acreage. They formed their group in 2002, after learning that someone had shot, cut, and gutted two horses. Since those murders, there have been a total of thirty known killings of these animals.

There are three hundred or so wild horses in the Sundre foothills. Bob and Doreen believe they carry traces of the Spanish mustangs brought to North America in the 1500s and cite an 1808 diary entry by explorer David Thompson describing the horses in the area. The Alberta government, however, asserts that the wild horses are descendants of domesticated equines from the turn of the twentieth century. Their official position is that the horses are not actually wild, but feral—domesticated animals that have gone un-tame and have intruded upon a land-scape. In other words, they're as foreign as the white men they helped settle this area.

Almost an hour into our drive, in Parker Ridge, about twenty-five miles from Banff National Park, Bob hits the brakes. "There's one in the woods," he says, as the car comes to a full stop on a logging road. "There's another."

I struggle to catch sight of them, but then the horses advance up through the grove of pine trees and squirt out onto the road, maybe a half-furlong in front of us.

We step outside the car. The horses, shaggy in their winter coats like plush animals, are shorter and smaller than the thoroughbreds I've become familiar with, but their chests are wider and their hindquarters are thicker. Wild horses travel in bands—a stallion, his harem of mares, and their foals—that rarely number over a dozen; they're often stalked by bachelor herds of young male horses that haven't yet started their own families. There are six horses in this band, including a foal.

The horses watch us with low-key curiosity, and as Bob takes photos with a zoom lens the size of a pepper grinder, I hide my moistening eyes behind my own camera. The band, following the lead of the boss mare, turn their backs towards us and run down the road, before melting into the forest again. The stallion, who will defend his band from bears, coyotes, wolves, and cougars, stays on the road, snorting and puffing at us.

"He's saying, 'Stand back,'" Doreen tells me. "'Keep away.'"

"They normally hang around longer," Bob says as the stallion leaves sight. "They're worried about the foal. But you can see how they will linger around people."

"We wish they were more distrustful," Doreen says. "They'd have a better chance of survival."

"How can anyone say they're not wild?" Bob asks me.

That day, we'll see a few more bands of horses, closer up and of varying numbers. We'll also pay our respects to the skeletal remains of a stallion murdered the previous December in a clearing by the road. For me, nothing underscores the difference between the so-called abuses at the racetrack and the undeniable cruelty of a wild animal murdered for pleasure than the sight of the slaughtered horse's tail lying on the other side of the road, carried and dropped there by a coyote.

And yet the image of that first band of horses rattles in my head for days afterwards. I was startled by the emotion that those horses inspired in me. At the sight of something so wonderful, I was reminded of the chain of events that led me here, beginning with my decision to buy a racehorse. If you asked me a year earlier what I'd be doing now, I'd never have guessed I'd be here. How could I?

⤳ 11 ⤶

THE ANIMAL COMMUNICATOR

NORMALLY, ON A Friday night race, Randi takes the day off from the post office to save herself a workday that runs from daybreak until midnight. But earlier that week she got into an argument with her supervisor for—*you won't fucking believe it*—swearing. Complaining about Randi swearing, of course, is like complaining about anyone else for blinking.

"I wasn't fucking swearing *at* him, just swearing, but he sent me to the principal's office," she explains to me before Blackie's race in her break room. "So I went to the doctor and he went, 'What do you want—stress leave?' We looked at the calendar and I said, 'September 5th.' And he said, 'Okay.' So, I didn't work today—and it was cool."

As Randi gets the horse ready, I return to the frontside to meet Harris and his family. Even while the stadium lights breathe away the darkness on the oval, there's still a ribbon of amber in the sky at Hastings. Typically, a summer night in the city is capped off with a cool breeze—cardigan weather for some—but this week in July the air is warm and flat.

Actually, it's Angie who shows up first, with Liam and Jack in tow. Jack, in seersucker shorts and a white T-shirt, keeps holding his mother's hand, because he's both fascinated by and terrified of the horses.

"He's been talking about coming here all week," Angie tells me, as her younger son, four, buries his head against her cardigan-wrapped waist, only to peek at the horses circling the paddock. "You know how shy he is, but he loves horses. And Liam's excited about betting."

Liam was initially promised a $5 wager on Blackie before successfully lawyering for the chance to bet on a race where he could actually pick the winner. The seven-year-old doesn't seem to take notice of the horses, but instead asks for my copy of the *Form*. "What are these numbers?" he asks, looking up from the broadsheet in the oversized nerd-scientist glasses that he insists on wearing. He points to a row of numbers in the statistics. "Here."

"The Beyer Speed number."

"What does that mean?" he asks.

The figure, which accounts for variables like track condition and rail biases, requires a complicated explanation that I cannot supply. "It says how fast the horse goes," I say instead.

He frowns at me, hoisting his lower lip the way his father does when paying the bill. "But if you know how fast the horse goes," he says, "then why doesn't everyone bet on the horse with the highest number?"

That's a question I'd like patiently and repeatedly explained myself. I could bumble through an overview of pace and trip handicapping, but I shudder in anticipation of the inevitable follow-up questions. "Well, there are other important factors to consider," I eventually say. "Like the shininess of the horses' coats, and the colour of the jockey's silks."

"You don't know, do you?"

"No," I say. "But do you guys want something to drink or a Popsicle?"

"Okay," he says in a tone that suggests that he will not be easily placated. "Do they have red-bean soup Fudgsicles?"

Jack pulls himself away from his mother to nod approvingly. "I want one, too."

I look to Angie, to see if they're kidding. Growing up, I felt that red-bean soup as a dessert was some kind of culturally sanctioned prank on Chinese children. Angie bounces back my puzzled face. "I have to drive half an hour out of my way to find red-bean treats," she tells me. "We live in a different age."

To the kids' visible disappointment, we settle for regular Popsicles, then slip into the paddock before Blackie's race. "What's keeping Harris?" I ask Angie.

"He's showing a house in Deep Cove," she explains.

"The market's picking up again," I say. It's a phrase that has begun to ping across the city like a chain letter.

"At least he's busy," she says. "Otherwise he gets existential."

The rapport I have with my friends' wives doesn't extend far beyond pleasantries. Give me two minutes, after all, and I'm waxing on about horse junk. For that reason, I'm not part of Angie and Harris's dinner-party circuit. As Angie watches Liam, who refuses to hold her hand in public, I grow anxious about the awkward silence looming ahead.

"Did Harris ever tell you my grandfather owned racehorses in Fort Erie?" she asks me. "I love horses."

The impression Harris gave me was that she disapproved of the sport. "I didn't know that."

"I kept telling Harris to buy into the horse with you, but he wouldn't. He thought he'd never get his money back."

"Oh."

She reads my face like a picture book. "Did he tell you a different story?"

I shake my head. "No."

"He did, *didn't he?*" She says "didn't he?" in a way that makes me feel like a squirming seven-year-old caught in a lie.

"Okay, yes," I admit. "He said you wouldn't let him buy into Blackie."

She shakes her head. "He's always blaming me for things."

"So," I say, recalling an earlier conversation, "does that also mean that you're *not* the one making him get a vasectomy?"

Angie ducks sheepishly. "Well, no—that one actually does fall on me. But my point still holds."

We watch Randi saddle Blackie and give her instructions to Perez. After her last victory, the mare has been bumped up to a higher price, $7,500. The reasoning behind this is that any horse who's claimed is placed in a "jail term," which means a horse's new owners are forced to race her one level above her purchase price for a month-long period—this keeps the owners of a claimed horse from immediately claiming that horse back at the same price, and then vice versa. The $7,500 level is a reasonable jump for a sharp horse like Blackie, but if she were purchased, she would need to race against horses at the $12,500 level, where she'd be outclassed; other trainers should know this and back off from the horse.

We leave the paddock to find a spot to watch the race. On the apron, by the eight pole—the pole that marks the point one furlong away from the finish line—I run into Nick, who's supposed to be at the football game scalping tickets for extra dough.

"Game just ended," he tells me.

"How did you do?"

"I made a hundred and seventy bucks. I just bought them off people on the street who had extra tickets. It's about three hours of work."

"Not bad," I say.

"Not bad," he repeats, folding his bottom lip up. At first he seems proud of his hourly wage, but as he chews the inside of his mouth, his face drops. "Well, it's not quite enough."

The gates flap out, and the horses bust through like drunks thrown out of a saloon. Coming out of the four hole, Blackie starts well, lying third at the clubhouse turn, with Angel Came Down, a horse who beat her earlier this year, out front. "Don't get goofy," Nick shouts to the horse. "Just sit there." The first quarter goes fast—22.2—as the pace horse stretches his lead to three lengths. "They're just flying up front. She's getting shuffled back, I guess." But Blackie hangs in there with the horse in second, Notis Me, and at the top of the turn, the three horses are knotted together like a bunch of bananas.

Angel Came Down starts running out of gas and Blackie is in second.

"Come on!" Nick screams. "Dig, dig!"

Perez lowers the reins on the horse, encouraging the colt to let loose, going to a half cross—holding the reins in one hand—and swatting the horse with his whip. His stance changes and he crouches lower. If a jockey just sits there with his lines dangling, he's a passenger. What a jockey does in the back half of the race, when the horse is "sent"—allowed to go full speed—is to physically *push* his horse and help him lengthen his stride. It's at this point that the rider stretches out from a "7" stance into a Superman flying mode. An analogy I read somewhere compares this motion to a child pumping his feet on a swing.

With Perez pushing her, Blackie seems to be gaining on Notis Me, who's racing inside, midway down the stretch. The two horses seem locked into each other, as though in a tango, neither wanting to cede ground to the other. But then another horse, Our Gin Girl, a relative long shot at thirteen to one, slingshots towards them on the outside. She moves beside Blackie, who looks surprised, thrown off by the interloper at her flank, and lets up on her acceleration.

"NOTIS ME, MOCHA TIME, HERE'S OUR GIN GIRL... OUR GIN GIRL TO SCORE."

I bet $10 across—win, place, and show—on Blackie, so make back part of my original bet. Liam shrewdly placed his $5 wager on the horse to show and actually turns a profit. Harris calls Angie to say he can't make it, so I bring his family into the backstretch without him, feeling too much like a substitute English teacher forced to lead a group of school kids, at the last minute, on a tour of a historic battleship—I'm not sure whether to say nothing or make things up. Jack's mouth hangs open at all the horses watching us from their stalls. Liam's excited about the easy cash in his hand.

As Blackie is hosed down and walked, Randi gives Jack and Liam carrots to feed the horses and introduces her current roster of horses. Unlike many trainers, who merely shorten a racehorse's longwinded official name in the barn, Randi takes pains to create personalized tags for her wards. There's Amy (a.k.a. Island Hopper Chopper), the horse in rehab (as in Amy Winehouse, who sang about going to a different kind of rehab); the Girl (Aubrey Road), a three-year-old filly brought in by Randi's friend Ardenne who stood funny when she first came in; Riley (Uncle Geno, named after Randi's Uncle Geno), whom Randi bred and owns outright, but who is injured and has never raced and stomps his front hoof all the time—"not because he's mean, but because he's bored"; May (Athena Estates), who was scratched from her most recent race because of a cough; and then Sylvester.

"I told my friend one time, 'Jesus, I'm going to have to go bankrupt and kill myself,' and the next day he won," Randi tells everyone. "He's made about a hundred grand. I like to think of him as the hero. But just not lately—right, Sylvester?"

The horse bobs his head like a Texas oil derrick, but settles down when I offer him a carrot. I like Sylvester a lot. Randi wonders whether his dip in performance isn't because the track's racing surface is harder than it has been in previous years or whether it's because the track has banned the use of hormones on horses for fear of negative publicity. (Randi insists that the steroids help the horses heal quickly and eat better.)

"Sylvester's always the hero," I tell everyone. "She's Randi's favourite."

As I say this, Alex brings Blackie back from around the centre aisle and into her shed, and all the attention turns to my horse, the pretty black mare who's run well enough to win, even if she fell short. The horse lets herself be patted, something she doesn't always do, and happily gobbles up the carrots that are offered to her, one by one. I turn to see Sylvester. How would it feel to be replaced as the hero, to be supplanted by a lesser horse having a better season? He's still whipping his head up and down, but no one notices anymore.

"There were many doubters as I strode against the moving walkway of conventional wisdom towards wealth, recognition, and immediate and delayed gratification. From this comes a prime lesson: never be afraid to try something that others may think is stupid or outlandishly weird.

If revenge is a dish best served cold, then innovation can be a swordfish crème brûlée. An innovator lets the end guide the means, even when those demands resemble a pregnant woman's cravings or an Iron Chef's fever dream.

It was with this attitude in mind that my racing endeavours brought me to a woman who claimed to speak to animals..."

FROM CHAPTER THREE, *The Winning Ticket Inside You*

Carole Serene is a tall woman with curly, reddish-brown hair cut just above her ears and has a warm, throaty laugh. When we meet outside the city at a fish and chips place by the water, halfway between her place and mine, she's wearing sandals, a houndstooth blouse, a long skirt, and black onyx jewellery. She breeds and trains Irish wolfhounds and belongs to a Jaguar car club. For her day job, she works for a food broker, putting a manufacturer's products into supermarkets. Before that, she worked in the pet food industry.

Since 1991, Carole Serene has also been a spiritual medium, channeller, and animal communicator. Her work, she tells me, is possible through the assistance of the spirit energy Seth, who first communicated through psychic Jane Roberts. Roberts, who "crossed over" in 1984, published the ancient spirit's channelled thoughts in a series of books known as the "Seth Material." Carole, whom I found online, transmits Seth's thoughts through a kind of automatic writing on pen and paper and has been looking for a publisher for her own channelled writings from the spirit energy—"It pertains to environmental issues of our time," she says—but when she wrote Roberts's publisher, she was sent a cease-and-desist letter.

"How can you copyright a spirit?" I ask her.

"Thank you. I rest my case," she tells me. "They claim that Seth said he'd never speak through anyone else. But Seth told *me* that he told her that he would never speak the words *he spoke to Jane Roberts* to another. So those topics are off the table, but we're dealing instead with today's environmental crisis."

Through Seth, Carole can offer guidance to people looking for answers to their personal problems. In a two-hour session, people will ask Seth questions, which he'll answer in writing by Carole's hand. "Sometimes, women come to find out when they will find Mr. Right," she tells me. "That's very shallow, but I understand it's important to them. So we address and move through that into what's really important to them in their lifetime. For some people, it's art—the fulfillment of their talents. We all have some talent, but we don't always have the confidence to share it with the world."

"And Seth has helped you find your calling in life?" I ask innocently.

Carole gives me the kind of encouraging, dumbfounded smile you'd offer someone who lets a beach ball of obviousness evade him. "*This* is my calling," she says. "I didn't know what I wanted to be when I grew up until Seth allowed me to be a channel through which to speak."

Seth seems to work in a couple of ways. He can upload his thoughts directly into Carole, but, when she helps people communicate with dead relatives or, more pertinently to me, animals, he's more of a go-between—like the operator who connects a collect caller to the recipient. Carole communicates with Seth, who gets hold of the animal and then fades into the background.

"They love the fact that somebody is there to talk to them about them," Carole tells me about the animals' reactions to her communications. As an example of her work, Carole tells me about communicating with a quarter horse whose owner was trying to get him to learn natural horsemanship, an approach to working with horses in which the animals get to make decisions. The quarter horse responded by being, at turns, aloof and belligerent. "It was very foreign to him. And this particular fellow said, 'I'm twenty years old. I'm an old guy. I just want her to leave me alone and let me do my work.' He also feels like he's failed and gets the anxiety that he'll be sent away."

"Horses have that anxiety?" I ask with some surprise. "In the racing world, that's a common reality."

"Horses don't live in the same homes very often. You'd be surprised by their sense of abandonment."

Carole's first conversation with an animal occurs without an actual meeting, though she likes to have a picture of the animal before her conversation. From her conversation, she then produces a transcript that she emails to the client. Although she normally charges $150 for the service, she's waived her fee for Blackie.

After my run-in with the Woman Who Hates Horseracing, I've come to Carole seeking assurance from Blackie that she actually wants to race. My view of psychics and the occult is they don't hurt. Even if it's all hokum, if you're prone to believing in such things, or even if you're not entirely disposed to not believing, it adds a confectioner's coating of significance to the meaningless Bundt cake of experience.

With a little prodding, I even convince Randi, who's profoundly skeptical about Carole's purported gift, to provide me with a couple of questions that she'd like answered by her mare: Does your right hock hurt? Does it hurt when you get near the end of the race or are you just tired?

But then, during our meeting, I think Carole's services might be used on Sylvester. After all, Blackie probably has gotten more attention than she deserves, and both Randi and I want to know why Sylvester is feeling so sluggish, whether it's not because of the lack of hormones. And since he's a gelding, I'd like to know, for empathetic male reasons, how he feels about that. He might not be the hero at the moment, but he's something better, at least in my opinion: complicated.

A FEW WEEKS after mentioning it, Nick gives me a copy of his writing assignment about the track. The essay starts at Santa Anita racecourse outside of Los Angeles. Sitting in the stands, he goes through the program and sees the names of trainers who've snatched some of racing's chunkiest pieces of silverware: the Triple Crown races, the Breeders' Cup, the Dubai World Cup. "Amongst all these familiar names was one that I was most familiar with," he writes, "but one that in this arena nobody else would recognize: my own."

Flashing back from this opening scene, Nick tells us about growing up as a devotee of the sport, reading everything he could find about horses. He picked up work as a hot walker at

Hastings, before getting his own trainer's licence. One wizened racetracker he met there warns him about the entrancing smell of horses: "He was right," Nick writes. "Once you are addicted to the smell, you crave it."

Eventually, Nick arrived in Los Angeles with Twanger, a horse with enormous talent despite his undistinguished pedigree, whom Nick had trained well enough to win every local stakes race. When Twanger first appeared at Santa Anita in November, the Mexican grooms at the stables had never before seen a horse with a winter coat. "Why do you bring a bear here?" one of them asked Nick. "[T]his is a place for the horse."

Coming from a piddling track in Canada, Nick's horse was so poorly regarded that no jockey was willing to ride him. "My head hung and I felt like a scolded child as I asked each rider's agent, and was given reason after reason why each rider would not take the mount," Nick writes. "I began to feel ill, I wanted to get into a warm bed, pull the covers over my head and disappear." Out of mercy, another trainer arranged for Twanger to be ridden by Laffit Pincay, Jr., one of the most successful jockeys ever, with 9,530 career wins.

Having trained Twanger for three months at Santa Anita, Nick is now in the stands to watch him make his racing debut in California. But even with Pincay aboard, Nick's horse quickly falls to the back of the pack—twelve lengths from the lead.

"What would I tell people, how could I excuse this?" Nick recalls himself thinking. "My eyes fell from the race. New shoes, black and uncreased. Why had I wasted money on these? Not to mention the new suit, shirt, and tie I was wearing. Who did I think I was? I was getting spanked for my arrogance."

At the turn, however, Twanger pours on speed. Pincay swats the horse with the whip, and the horse, nostrils flaring and ears pinned back, responds instantly. The horse begins to make ground, picking off the favourites and closing in on the leader when they reach the finish line. Twanger comes in a close second.

Overjoyed, Nick runs into the unsaddling area of the track, where he takes hold of his horse, who's covered with dirt and sweat. Pincay dismounts and shakes his hand.

"Nice horse . . . He ran real big, man," Nick recalls the Panama-born rider telling him. "I want to ride him again . . . anytime soon."

The essay, while florid at times, is well written. I've kept reading because the version of Nick has a real stake in the story—unlike the stuff I write, with its ambivalent narrators who are too cautious to bet it all. And in this piece, I see another version of Nick, someone who was in thrall to racing's beauty and history. Nowadays, he seems more keenly aware of the racing world's pragmatic realities. He cares about his work as an agent and a trainer, and yet he seems at a remove from it, maybe because he needs to scalp tickets for extra money. The racetrack might provide a job and a way of life, but it's no longer a path to glory.

I want the story to end on a note of near-triumph, with Twanger's near-victory. Even if Nick and Twanger don't take over Santa Anita, I want to see them both leave with no regrets.

But Twanger is sent back to Vancouver. Nick lingers in Los Angeles for two more years until visa restrictions force him back north. Upon his return, he finds Hastings harmed by new competition from casinos being built around the city. Fewer horses are being bred, purses have been cut, racing schedules shortened. And yet Nick can't kick his addiction to that smell.

I see him a few weeks later at the casino, sitting behind an Egyptian-themed slot machine that flashes hieroglyphics in place of cherries. He smiles when I tell him how much I like the essay, but doesn't take his eyes off the screen.

"Whatever happened to Twanger?" I ask him about his horse, who still holds a track record for stakes wins.

"The owner bred him locally for a while, but he wasn't successful as a stud," Nick says. "So he started racing again and broke down in a race in Seattle."

I wish I never asked.

Nick presses a button at the bottom of the machine and hieroglyphs start spinning again.

"How are you doing on the slots?" I ask him, nodding towards the screen.

"Not bad today. I'm up a couple hundred bucks."

"That's pretty good."

"It's a stupid thing to do."

Our conversation trails off, and he returns his attention wholly to the flashing, chiming machine. I wonder what kind of smell it gives off.

A COUPLE OF weeks later, I find a voice mail from Nick. "I'm calling with regard to Mocha Time," he says in a clipped message. "Please give me a call back."

The first thought I have is that the horse is injured, and I'm lightheaded as I dial his number. But Nick tells me that a couple of Blackie's owners, people I've met only in passing, have suddenly decided they no longer want to be her owner. "Now we're trying to figure out what to do with the horse," Nick says. "Randi told me to handle it."

"What are the options?" I ask.

"Well, I'm trying to figure it out," he says. "The way it is now, Randi owns ninety percent of the horse, and that means not enough money is coming in regularly. We could sell the horse privately or race her low enough that she gets claimed."

As Nick discusses the options, I recall a conversation I had with my father a few days ago. I was at my parents' house, watching TV, when he walked into the room and asked about my horse. I mentioned her last race and suggested she'd be racing again in a couple of weeks.

"That's too bad," he said, "I'll be out of town."

"Oh," I said. "I wish you could make it."

"Have I ever told you of the friend I have in Hong Kong?" he asked me, settling into the armchair next to the couch. "He's a really wealthy guy and owned a lot of racehorses. But he had one horse that he just *loved*. It was his favourite horse." My father smiled at the memory. "There's so little land in Hong Kong that there are no places to send horses to after they finish racing, so when that horse retired, my friend sent it to a stable in New Zealand. But he missed seeing the horse, so he decided to buy a winery there to have an excuse to visit him."

There's a pause on the phone between Nick and me. I feel as though I should volunteer to write a cheque. But until then, I thought I was only involved with the horse for the year, with an option for the next season. Nick has never called me before; until now, I've never felt greasy dealing with him, as though he were calibrating his words, or that I needed to be wary of him. Here and now, he's become cagey. What are the chances I'll see this money back?

Then again, why shouldn't Nick ask me for a cheque? I've spent the summer treating the horse's accomplishments, and the efforts of her trainer, as my own. Now I'm called upon to do the one thing an owner does, write a cheque, but am tripped up by my distrust and ambivalence.

This is, in my mind, a test of character. Will I act cautiously, on the assumption that all racetrackers are charlatans—or will I follow my passion and give my new friends a chance? Am I like the besotted owner my father described, someone whose attachment to an animal leads him to behave in a way that's not altogether expedient, or am I an owner only according to the paperwork, a tourist to horseracing, a guy with no true stake in this world—no true stake in any world?

With all that in mind, I offer to double my stake in Blackie.

Nick asks me to meet him at the track with another cheque. Before I leave, I dial Randi's number.

"I knew you'd be calling me," she says. I can hear her huffing as she does her route.

"Is it okay for me to write Nick a cheque?" I ask.

"Probably," she says, cackling. "Well, I think it should be cool."

"That's a relief."

"I won't let you get fucked," she says. "Besides, this will give you a taste of what it's like to be in horseracing as an owner. You don't namby-pamby around."

The amount of my money I invested was a sum that I was comfortable to part with; twice that much, without any promise of a return, is a different matter. Driving to the track, I think about how easy it could be for someone like me to be swindled by a racetracker. Then I tell myself that neither Randi nor Nick has ever been dishonest with me; I have no reason to distrust them—not yet.

At Hastings, I look for Nick at the track bar, Jerome's, but don't see him. Naturally, I head straight to the casino, where I expect him to be pouring his cash—and maybe my own—into a machine. I find him instead outside the other, upper-floor entrance to Jerome's and we settle at a table in the bar. It's an off-day at the track, and the basement bar is filled only with the punters watching simulcasts from other tracks.

"I really appreciate this," he says. "You're helping us out of a jam."

"Sure," I say evenly. "Do I make the cheque to you or Randi?"

"You can make it out to me."

I flinch.

"Did you bring a receipt?" I ask as I fill out the cheque.

"Oh. No," he says. "I forgot."

I don't mention that an hour ago, when we arranged to meet, he promised to put together a receipt. He borrows a strip of cash-register ribbon from behind the bar and quickly makes out a handwritten receipt for me and I return home, still unsure about my decision.

Before the day ends, a cashier at Money Mart calls me to verify the cheque I've just written. Nick's urgency to take my money isn't reassuring. To calm myself down, I sit in front of my laptop and start another pretend how-to book, *What I Learned at the Track: A Manual of Failure*.

LESSON ONE: Write a Cheque

Racetrackers had just bled several thousand dollars away from me after I went headlong into an expensive sport that I knew little about. I had purchased a racehorse to intentionally expose myself to a level of risk and commitment that I had so steadfastly avoided throughout my life. I hoped to show I was not the person I'd spent my life being.

This ultimately proved to be the point where my life completely unravelled. From here, I lost all the money I'd saved, fell into a slough of despair that left me unable to work for months and, out of shock, lost my ability to feel pain or smell, and then briefly dabbled in cocaine and sweater vests.

After signing away money that I wouldn't get back, I should have run far, far away. I should have been content with my limitations, happy to be emotionally standoffish and self-contained, but in spite of this failure, I needed to poke and prod, to double down. Horseracing is described in an old movie as "a slow poison." I let this toxic sport destroy me, slowly but fully.

This is my sad story...

12

SID MARTIN, PART TWO

BACK IN STABLE A, Alex's mood shoots up and down like a gunfight on a Ferris wheel. When he's grumpy, he's mute and unwilling to make eye contact. He and Randi feud throughout that summer, with Alex griping about money he feels she owes him. But in the past couple of weeks, his spirits have improved for two reasons. Reason one, the main reason, is that his twenty-year-old son Shawn arrived from Cloverdale, where the harness-racing track is located.

If people like Randi wind up at the track out of some absence in their own family life, there seem to be at least as many people here because of family connections, people who work with horses because their parents taught them how. My imagination congeals and scabs over trying to imagine Alex as a father, and yet he fawns over his son, whom he raised on his own without any evident catastrophe. Shawn's a friendly, polite guy, stoutly constructed, with a closely shaven head, a round, pale face. Like his dad, he walks horses around the stables and the paddock, and lives in a tack room, twenty feet from Alex. For dinner, the two of them eat tuna fish sandwiches and tomato soup to save their money for wagers, which brings us to reason two for Alex's buoyancy.

Alex scored big last week on a triactor bet on a simulcast race from Saratoga with the lucky numbers supplied by his dead wife. "Shawn is sleeping and I said I need someone to guard this fucking seat, and I comes running here, and I find Shawn," he tells me, his eyes glinting, on the day Sylvester runs his first race in two months. "'Mummy says to bet 2–3–6,' I tell him. She says, 'Box it, Daddy.' I won $800 on the race in Saratoga. The 2–3–6 starts, and you can bet any fucking track. It's a spiritual thing. The point of it is you have to be consistent. Shawn's mother is now a saint. People don't talk to you from hell. They talk to you from heaven."

I ask Alex, whose wife died when Shawn was four, how often she talks to him from the spirit world.

"Well, when she died on a Tuesday, she started talking to us on Thursday night." His eyes suddenly brim with feeling. "She died of criminal negligence by the doctors," he says, glancing away in disgust. "The hospital says, 'We can cure your lung cancer if you come down to the hospital on Tuesday—you'll be cured by Thursday.' Thursday they called us to say she burned to death in a radiation chamber. It was an accident; it was turned too high."

A FEW DAYS after our first meeting, on a special mid-week, Canada Day race day, I watch Sid Martin prepare one of his horses, A Cut Above, for the first sprint. Martin's wearing a latte-coloured turtleneck, a red cap, a pressed jacket, and aqua-coloured slacks. Other trainers, in comparison, work in jeans and short-sleeved plaid shirts and ball caps. Martin's actually dressed down compared with some of the winner's photos I've seen, even those from a few years ago, in which he looks like an *Ocean's Eleven* extra in a black suit and skinny black tie, a cigarette in his hand.

In a paddock stall, Martin places the cloth under the saddle and adjusts the horse's bridle. He notices me and points to the island of lawn where visitors linger in the paddock. "Stand back," he says. "You're safer there."

When the horse is saddled, he ambles over to me, shaking my hand. I ask him how he thinks the horse will do, which I'm quickly learning is a pointless, if not stupid, question to ask a trainer or owner before a race. Martin gives me the same kind of answer Randi gives me about her horses. "I can't let you know until after the race," he says in his muted mumble. "She looked fine this morning, but she's probably the longest shot on the board."

At his busiest in California, Martin had twenty horses at Hollywood Park and twenty at Santa Anita. "I used to say if that's success, I don't want it," he told me when we first met. "I had ulcers, kidney stones, hemorrhoids. They're all behind me now." After twenty years in California—in his opinion, "the best twenty years of racing ever"—Martin returned to Canada and Hastings Park (then called Exhibition Park) in 1986. "I missed the seasons," he said. Although he was semi-retired, Martin was active enough to be the second leading trainer in 1990, the year he was inducted into the B.C. Horse Racing Hall of Fame, and win the B.C. Derby with Flying Sauce in 1995. This year, however, has been tough, with only one win coming early in the season.

Martin's jockey for the race, Giovanni Franco, comes to receive his instructions. Because of the multitude of variables in a race, the trainer's advice often needs to be disregarded by a jockey, whose own good judgment takes precedence. A trainer's advice is, thus, delivered offhandedly, in the same imprecise, encouraging manner you would direct your house-sitter to water the plants.

"Don't push too hard if you're going head-to-head, you know what I mean?" says Martin, who's worried about the language barrier with Franco. About half the jockey's colony at Hastings is Mexican, and while the more veteran riders speak good English, the younger ones often get by with nodding and smiling. "Just get comfortable."

Martin suggests that we watch the race from his box seat. As we step out of the paddock, he hands me a folded piece of paper. "This was from Glen," he mumbles. "It's a poem."

I found out about the murdered son of Sid Martin a few days after our initial meeting, and had been seeking a tactful way to broach the subject. Now with this opportunity hand-delivered by Martin himself, I follow the racing legend to the stands, watching his feet pedal in a sprightly manner as he jogs up the steps to the clubhouse boxes. As usual, people nod and call out his name. We sit down at a box already occupied by another friend of Sid's, someone whose name I now forget.

Martin plucks a cigarette from his shirt pocket. "I'm just going to light this," he says, smiling. "It's illegal, but what the heck."

The gates open. With Franco on him in Day-Glo orange silks, A Cut Above takes the lead going into the clubhouse turn, but he falls to second, then third, in the backstretch, and by the time they reach the top of the lane, he's passed by the rest of the field. Martin watches, leaning forward on the railing of the box seat. His expression is all mass, no motion. The eyes are still narrowed, his bottom lip flat as a horseshoe.

"He was in a little tough," he says after a drawn-out pause. "If he hits a sloppy track, it's gangbusters."

LATER, READING Glen's poem, it occurs to me that, even when you choose to fight with your father, you do so on his terms. It's your father who picks the rules for you to break, each one of them another plot point in his unlived life.

In many ways, Sid Martin's oldest son seemed to conscientiously refute his father's clean-cut, soft-spoken example. From what I've been told, Glen was boisterous, overly generous, and social. He also dealt drugs at the track, which led to his death. It's worth nothing, however, that even while he was rattling his father's well-being, he was doing it at the place they both loved.

Glen's poem, written for his father in honour of his return from California, shows him in a more unctuous mood:

At FIFTY-SIX, You've made your mark!
So now you're back at Exhibition Park!
Settled down, semi-retirement is due!
I know Vancouver is home to you.

Your friends and relatives all are there!
People like you we all find rare!

I have come to respect you for the man you are
Following your advice will take a man far!

A good reputation, honesty and class
Those are traits, I hope you have passed.

Learning by examples, that you set
I've followed your lead, on that you can bet.

Now that I'm older, my feelings have grown
Your philosophies are followed, I call them my own.

So as you look back on your cherished past...
Realize the teachings, your shadow has cast.

Your influence has not been lost.
I'm also a survivor, no matter the cost.

I value the knowledge you have imparted
A good foundation for me to get started.

In the future, you will see
The effect your training has had on me.

For what you stand for, I believe!
And that I will follow until I succeed.

I'm always proud to be your son
To me you are considered #1!

On your birthday, I hope you are glad
Receiving this poem about my Gemini Dad.

"Glenny was a sweet guy," Randi tells me in her break room after I watch Sid's race. The track simulcast plays on her TV. "It's sad he's gone. He was always wanting to please his dad. I think that's why he got his trainer's licence. But he was a good horseman, too."

"So he and Sid didn't get along?" I ask her.

"I wouldn't say that, don't put any fucking words in my mouth."

"I didn't know how to bring up Glen," I tell her. "I wasn't sure Sid wanted to talk about him."

"Until last year, he used to have his stalls up in this barn and he would come by and talk about Glen. He must miss him a lot."

If Martin has been welcomed into racing's most glorious precincts, the death of his son acquaints him with its seamy side, the part that comes in tow with the track's transient workforce and their happy-sad, feast-or-famine lifestyle. That season, I hear about one exercise rider who's suspended for thirty days for using cocaine and another gallop boy who blamed a rival trainer for slipping drugs into him. Hastings has its own addiction counsellor and weekly Alcoholics Anonymous meetings. It also has random drug tests that are routinely administered to backstretch workers, swabs that can be used to track any narcotics use in the previous four days. The testing doesn't seem to derive from any desire to enforce morality or improve workplace safety so much as to pick off the sketchiest personalities.

The temptations that Sid successfully avoided were the same that pulled his son under. In November 2002, Glen and his girlfriend, Julie Smith, were gunned down. Their bodies were left in the trunk of Glen's abandoned car and discovered two days later when it was impounded. Almost five years later, a former jockey's agent named Michael Joseph Wilson was convicted of two counts of first-degree murder. "Parents, siblings and friends of the deceased wept—as did Wilson's supporters—as B.C. Supreme Court Justice Donna Martinson read her verdict," wrote Susan Lazaruk in the *Province* in 2007. Later, Lazaruk wrote that "Martin was shot at close range six times, Smith 11 times, and both were hit in the head with a hammer. Smith, [who] was 'in the wrong place at the wrong time,' also was stabbed in the leg and garrotted with a wire."

According to the article in the *Province*, Wilson was caught by the RCMP in a "Mr. Big sting." Undercover Mounties, posing as gangsters, egged Wilson to admit to a past crime to prove himself badass enough to join their ranks. In court, Wilson claimed he exaggerated his role to the undercover cops and fingered another track figure, his uncle Mark Patzer, a one-time leading jockey at Hastings, as the actual killer.

The Crown prosecutor asserted that the younger Martin, who was forty-eight when he died, owned a marijuana grow op in a farmhouse he leased outside the city in Pitt Meadows. Wilson lived in the house and ran the grow op with Patzer. Glen became unhappy with their partnership, which angered Wilson and Patzer enough that his life had to end. Wilson insisted that he wasn't the triggerman, that he lent his pistol to his uncle, who killed Martin and Smith. According to Wilson, Patzer killed Sid Martin's son first in the lower level of the house. Wilson was with Smith upstairs, with the television's volume turned up to obscure the noise of the killing. Patzer then called Wilson on his cell phone to bring Smith down.

Although he was declared a suspect, Patzer has never been arrested for the murder. Wilson testified that he was only guilty of disposing of their bodies, which his uncle forced him to do. But he also told the RCMP that immediately after the killing "he bought a CD by Papa Roach, with its title track, 'Getting Away with Murder.'"

"Asked by the undercover officer why the slaying happened," Keith Fraser reports in another article in the *Province*, "Wilson told him that he and his uncle were concerned about the reputation of the track."

THE NEXT TIME I meet with Sid Martin, I bring my laptop to Trackers's patio, where he's waiting with a fresh cigarette ready. Martin said he's never seen a replay of his Triple Crown, so I found them all online and downloaded them for him. Randi happens to come across us while she's sipping a bottle of iced tea. "Having fun with my friend here?" she asks him as they light up their cigarettes in tandem.

We squint at the video. The video resolution is low and the glare from sitting outside washes out the screen.

"Is this the Derby?" Randi asks.

I nod.

She turns to Martin. "Brings back old memories?"

"Not good ones," he says.

We get to the point where Diabolo and Avatar are running neck and neck. Avatar would go on to win the Belmont. After surgery to repair a shattered pastern, Diabolo was put to stud in Arkansas. Martin studies the race with the same stoic concentration that he did watching A Cut Above race a week earlier.

"Oh, look, you're fucking out in front," Randi says.

A few racetrackers have gathered around us. "Is this You-Tube?" one guy in a train conductor's cap asks. "I've got a video for you after this."

"This is when Sid's horse gets bumped," I say to Randi as the video shows the race at the final turn.

"Yeah, he did get fucking bumped. You still did fucking good," she tells Martin. "Let's watch the one where Forego beat Honest Pleasure in the Marlboro Cup."

"Just punch in Silky Sullivan," says the guy in the cap.

After the crowd loses interest, Martin is even more laconic than usual, and I realize maybe I got it wrong. I thought that someone who kept such thick scrapbooks of the past would be eager to return to it, but it could be those records are Martin's way of flash-freezing that time, locking those memories down with the exception of a few pre-made anecdotes and quips. Or maybe it makes for a better story to tell everyone you've never seen a replay in all these years. Who am I to squelch this lie of convenience?

Martin flips open his pack of cigarettes at the table, but finds it empty. Without a second of panic, he replaces it with another pack from his shirt pocket. "Do you smoke?" he asks me.

"Sometimes when I drink."

"Try one of these. I've got lots of smokes."

As I try to keep from coughing, I bring up the poem that Glen wrote for him. The register of Martin's voice drops fractionally, growing slightly more hoarse.

"It was the last thing that should have happened to him because he was the most generous man; everyone liked him," says Martin, who has three other children, about Glen's murder. "The last thing he deserved. He'd drive across town because so-and-so needed a chair. He'd have barbecues here, and it was all on his own dime. I used to say, 'If I had one of your friends, I wouldn't need enemies.' They were down-and-outers, but he overlooked it."

Martin was aware of his son's involvement with drugs since the early eighties, when he was forced to spring Glen out of jail after being held for drug charges in Mexico. He dismisses his son's marijuana dealing as a game. "If he ever made anything, he'd give it all away," he says. "He was hyper, and he said the marijuana calmed him. He was really a good horseman. When he was eight in school, he had some baby chicks. He put them in a cardboard box. In the cardboard, he made lanes and had the kids come after school betting on the chicks to race. He wrote up a racing form. It was perfect." Martin's eyes crinkle the way they do when he tells his jokes.

Glen Martin got his trainer's licence in 1999 and won his first race early in the season. A *Province* article written by Tom Harrison describes the younger Martin as "a man who is full of life with plenty of well-earned chutzpa and tonnes of confidence." The article also hints at his tenuous relationship with his father. "For years, my dad would tell everyone he would have a good day if I was not on *America's Most Wanted*," he's quoted as saying. "It took awhile for both of us, but I feel he is very proud right now."

Only three years afterwards, he was found dead. "A person doesn't understand unless you go through it," Sid says. In the first few summers following his son's murder, Martin trained in Winnipeg, where he galloped horses forty years ago, to escape any reminders of Glen at Hastings. He was right to do so. Wilson, who was a jockey's agent as late as 2004, would have breezed past Sid in his barn as he hustled mounts for his rider. Your stomach turns on Martin's behalf.

"He never walked through *my* barn," Martin says defiantly. "I saw him from a distance and I could tell he was a scumbag from a hundred and fifty feet away."

The horses, as usual, have been Martin's consolation, even if this year hasn't been fruitful. "It costs you an arm and a leg to keep in the game," he says. "I'll reduce down to one by the end of the meet. I think this filly could be worth keeping. I really don't see myself retiring." He shakes his head emphatically. "I'd be bored sick in a week if I didn't have something to do."

From the same pocket where he kept his extra smokes, Martin brings out his most recent newspaper clipping, this one written a few years ago when he was at Assiniboia Downs in Winnipeg.

I glance at the article and see a quote I like. "'You give a year-ling to a sick man and he'll live forever,'" I read back to him. "Did you make that up?"

"It's an old adage. It's the best therapy in the world to be involved with horses. It's like family down here."

AFTER LUNCH, crossing the backside to the parking lot, I catch sight of actual family. Alex and Shawn are walking towards the gambling floor with the kind of deliberate, patient tread you develop when you make your living trading strides with twelve-hundred-pound quadrupeds. To my eyes, father and son regard each other mindfully, each of them treating the other as though he were the high-priced and fragile creature who demands care and protection.

Martin doesn't notice. At the parking lot, when I remove the box of scrapbooks from my car, he insists again on accepting the load himself. A man his age doesn't need to prove his strength. But then that box contains his clippings and his winner's photos, every professional high point as witnessed by others—a notarization of a life's worthiness. It must feel good to carry that weight.

⤳ 13 ⤶

~~GET A TATTOO~~

LESSON TWO: Be Low Maintenance.

It's Christmas night, 2045. I sit in my basement suite alone, eating fancy-grade cat food—it's a holiday, after all—as my second-hand hologram player shows a pornographic cooking program. No one has called me or sent me a neuro-transmitted holiday greeting, except for my sponsor at Gamblers Anonymous.

I am without friends. It was around my time at the racetrack that I coined and subscribed to this new adage: Friendships are acts of consensual psychological and emotional nipple-twisting. We deliver and sustain small doses of neglect and abuse. That was how I alienated everyone.

Before that, I always felt as though I were an exemplary friend: generous, convivial, and a fun drunk. Most of all, I was low maintenance. I didn't expect much from my friends with the implicit understanding that they shouldn't expect much from me. What I ultimately learned was the harm one could inflict by doing nothing at all and refusing to engage.

FROM *WHAT I LEARNED AT THE TRACK:*
A Manual of Failure

Hanging around the backside, I've been dreading my next run-in with Kulwant. Since our get-together, he's left two unanswered voice mails and emailed me an unreadable op-ed piece about global poverty in hopes that I can help him get it published. At Trackers, where I'm buying a coffee, and some apples and bananas for Randi's horses, I find him sitting alone with a chicken burger and a beer. A library copy of Roberto Bolaño's *Nazi Literature in the Americas* sits in front of him, opened and faced down.

My first impulse is to run away, but these encounters will continue in the future. The best course of action, then, is to finesse myself through the awkwardness. Failing that, I'll take a body splash into said awkwardness.

"Hey, I've been looking for you," I say with faux cheer. "Mind if I sit?"

He looks up, taking a bite of his burger before saying a word. He's wearing a T-shirt, and I notice, for the first time, the etched muscle in his forearms; groom work has transformed him into the wiry proletariat he's always fancied himself to be. "You'd honour me," he mumbles through his half-chewed lunch.

I apologize for not returning his calls and mention I'll need to read his commentary again. "I've been out of town a lot," I say, "and doing, like, a hundred things all at once."

"Dilettantes don't have it easy," he says. "I cleaned up horse-shit for the 393rd consecutive work day, then someone bought the used van I wanted to buy, which would have been my ticket out of the tack room. But your life—now that's hard."

In years past, I would pay back the sarcasm. Perhaps it's some newfound maturity, or my old-found emotional distance, that lets me shrug it off. This seems only to infuriate Kulwant further. "So, how's your little bottom claimer?" he asks me.

I perk up. "Good, which is why we don't like the layoff," I say. "I'm lucky to have"—and here I throw him a term I picked up from the *Form*—"such an honest runner."

"Huh," he says. "Once you get bored of thoroughbreds, what's going to be your next manly passion? Omaha Hi-Lo? Small batch ryes? Don't tell me you don't have something lined up already."

"Actually, there are some great new ryes coming out of—" I say, before reconsidering. "I need to go."

He looks over his shoulder as I exit. "Have fun, horseman."

KULWANT ISN'T the only friend I've pushed away, although in Harris's case it's done more unwittingly. My first inkling that he might be miffed comes when he doesn't attend Blackie's race with his family. Later, I don't hear from him about plans we made earlier in the month to see a show by a band we both liked in the nineties. At first, I decide to let it drop. Friendships, after all, benefit from their fallow periods, and I wear people down, over extended periods, with my standoffishness and crotchety ambivalence. But then again, I really want to see this band play, and no one else will come.

On the only free day I have, a Sunday, I find out through Angie that Harris is working an open house on the east side. The condo is located in a building with a speckled brick facade; the patio decks of the units facing the street are stuffed with unused exercise equipment and storage bins. It is immediately recognizable. Harris buzzes me in.

The elevator takes me to the third floor, where a muscle-memory makes me turn right towards the end of the hallway with the burnt-out light. Liam lets me in, and then runs back to his brother. The apartment is furnished more sparingly than my previous visit here. As I enter, one young couple is leaving the place with an information sheet.

"Wasn't I supposed to buy this place?" I ask.

"Yeah, in February," Harris says, handing me a printout. "Make me an offer. The price has been dropped by twenty grand."

The condo was taken off the market in the spring and listed

again, through Harris, in July. Jack and Liam are whispering to each other in the windowless "flex space" that I was expected to slide my desk into.

"What are they up to?" Harris asks.

When we open the mirrored, folding door, we find them each under a box. Harris hoists one box and finds Liam crouched on the floor.

"What are you guys doing?" I ask him in a patronizing kid's voice.

"Pretending," Liam says.

"What are you pretending to be?"

Liam starts scratching his arms. "Bedbugs."

Jack lifts up one side of his box.

"We're bedbugs," he screams. "You have to burn all your clothes!"

The open house ends. Afterwards, before it gets dark, we escort the kids to the park across the street and watch them take turns on the slide. "So, why didn't you come to the track the other day?" I ask.

Harris sighs, stretching out his feet as he leans into the bench. "I don't know," he says. "I had a client, and it's a hassle, and I mean, what's the big deal—am I your lucky charm?"

"What's wrong?" I ask him.

"Well, I have an appointment for a vasectomy upcoming, and now I'm stuck selling a bedbug-infested shithole."

I give him the stink-eye. "You told me it was a 'cozy entry-level unit.' You were lying, weren't you?"

"Let me ask you this," he says. "Was my book that bad that you couldn't say anything about it?"

I'd promised, for the third time, to read it a month ago, but again I found other, more pressing work. In reality, the idea that Harris—who, already in my mind, had enough—could write a decent book pissed me off.

"Actually..." I begin.

As I confess, Harris's lower lip begins trembling. "What is wrong with you?" he asks me. "You know this is important to me."

"I know."

"I've waited months."

"Well, I've spent almost a decade trying to write my second novel," I say. "It's like my personal Iraq War."

"Oh, that's hilarious," he says. "Why does it always have to be about you and your multitude of hang-ups?"

Harris only lets up on me when Jack and Liam stop running around the tire swing and begin watching us. We smile and wave at the kids, who take their time getting back to their circuit. Liam calls their race like the announcer at Hastings— they're at the finish line when he edges out his overmatched younger brother at the wire. "It's Mocha Time to score!" Liam screams. Jack doubles over, his cheeks pink.

RANDI'S FIFTIETH BIRTHDAY falls on July 31, three days prior to my thirty-fourth. "Before we all got too tired," Randi says, "I used to be in charge of finding fun things to do. One time we rented a limo on my fortieth birthday, or at least people thought it was my fortieth. Another time we had a girls' shower party for getting married and we rented a bus. It was my idea—it was so stupid. We met at the track and made everyone pay, like, ten dollars, and then we went to a bunch of bars. Then some girls met some guys and took them on the bus. It was kind of a blur. We were dancing on the table in a bar downtown."

"You're dancing on the table in a lot of your old stories," I tell her. The previous week she told me about dancing on a table in Mexico, to "Enter Sandman" by Metallica.

"I know, I used to do that a lot."

"Was 'Enter Sandman' playing?"

"No, my stripping song is AC/DC's 'You Shook Me All Night Long.'" She sings the song's opening line: *"She was a fast machine / She kept the motor clean."*

I finished the line for her and we bobbed our heads in unison: *"She was the best damn woman that I ever seen."*

A few weeks earlier, we agreed to get tattoos on her birthday from one of Randi's exercise riders, Cenek, who does tattoo art as a hobby. Randi still seems keen on the idea.

"I could get something writing-related to remind me of you," she tells me. "Like a pen."

"Ugh," I say. "Why don't you just get a panda bear? It's hairy and Chinese."

"And you could get a picture of Blackie on your arm."

"Yeah, but I bet she'd get claimed the next day," I say. As much as I like my horse, I'm not sure she's arm-worthy. "I was thinking a Triple Crown winner, or maybe a champion—like Barbaro."

Randi wrinkles her nose. "Really, why would you want that?"

Because of my dithering, Randi's birthday goes by un-tattooed. Instead, her friends drop by the shed row bearing cake and gifts. Alex, who normally gets $100 from Randi for his birthday, decides to give her a C-note with the stipulation that she use the money to wager on "Mummy's numbers"; one summer afternoon, they spend the day betting 2–3–6 triactors. I bring her a plush pillow made to look like a horse's head—as in the scene in *The Godfather* where Don Corleone has the severed head of a racehorse placed in the bed of an enemy as a breakfast-time surprise. It gets a laugh.

I step outside to say hello to Blackie. Her head is jutting out of her stall, but when she catches sight of me, she ducks her head inside. I peek in; she is munching hay.

"You know what?" I say to Blackie. "This is getting old."

She turns back to me; I must have caught her attention.

"I've already doubled my share in you," I continue. "I don't expect you to fall over me with appreciation. But I wouldn't mind it if you acted as though you didn't hate me."

The horse does a three-point turn in her stall, and I back away as she pokes her head out. Her ears are pricked eagerly.

"I'm glad we talked this through," I say. "Who cares if people think it's stupid to talk to a horse?"

When I reach out to stroke her neck, Blackie bites my arm. Whimpering, I rub it as she returns inside to graze on her hay bale in peace.

SINCE SHE'S NOT at the post office, I imagine Randi would be in a better mood on my visits. But when I follow her on her mail route, she's glad to have company. When I show up to the stable while she's working, even with my *enhanced* stake in her horse, I'm nothing but a nuisance.

"You always pick the worst times to show up," she tells me one morning. "I can't talk."

"That's okay," I say, disappearing into the break room to read a book.

A few minutes later, she comes into the room looking for her cigarettes. "I can't answer no fucking questions," she says.

"I'm not asking any," I say, holding up my hands in protest.

A couple of minutes later, I see Nick pass by, his face shadowed as he seeks out Randi. Their argument involves a horse that Nick entered for Randi in a race that features an overwhelming favourite.

"Just once," I hear Randi yell, "I would like you to listen to me."

"The race is in two days," he says back. "There's no reason to let it ruin your mood for that long."

"I mean, we're just running for the second-place money."

"I can't fucking look at you. Stupid cow."

I see Nick storming by in the other direction.

Randi returns to the break room. "I can't have you here right now," she says.

"I'm not saying anything."

"I know, but I just want to be alone."

As far as I can tell, Randi hates being alone. Once or twice, after I go on her route with her, she'll cajole me into helping her feed the horses, because the stables are pretty empty in the afternoon. And if we're parked in different lots at the track, she'll ask me for a ride because she doesn't want to walk alone.

I tell myself that verbal abuse from Randi is a by-product of her affection. I tell myself that big boys don't let mean ladies hurt their feelings. It doesn't work.

So I avoid the front- and backsides for a week, only returning to cheer on Sylvester, who's racing at his lowest-ever price, $17,500. The favourite in the race is Distorted Glamour, a five-year-old California-bred gelding who's the wastrel trust-fund brat of the field. According to the *Form*, he was sired by Distorted Humor for $150,000; by comparison, the stud fee for Sylvester's dad was $4,000 and none of the other entries in the six-horse field were sired for more than $30,000. And yet the horse only has lifetime earnings of $29,732—less than a third of Sylvester's earnings.

Wearing white blinkers and starting on the outside, Sylvester begins well, moving inside and sitting second behind Distorted Glamour, who builds his lead in the far turn. Coming down the stretch, Sylvester manages to hang on for third.

I win some money on Sylvester, but my gambling day limps on in misery. I try to make back my losses on the final race on a card, a mile-and-an-eighth route where the two and three horses are heavily favoured; and I like the five-horse because Dave Wilson, who rode the horse to second place in his previous race, is on him again. The guy sitting next to me tells me to go for the six-horse.

The six-horse, who's actually the third-favourite in the race, doesn't look bad but I like the five-horse more and make a show bet on him and then a $2 2–3–5 triactor bet. It's only after I've placed a wager, and the horses are in the gate at the top of the far stretch, that I realize that Alex's numbers, 2–3–6, are actually the favoured horses.

Of course, 2–3–6 wins. I gather enough courage to return to the backstretch and run into Randi in a stall with Sylvester.

"There you are," she said. "I was wondering where you were. I thought I'd scared you off the other day."

"What are you talking about?" I say, feigning nonchalance as I pet Sylvester, whose eyes look bloodshot. "Did you see Alex's numbers pay out in the eighth race?"

Randi laughs. "Yeah, but they were the favourites."

"*Still,*" I say. "What's wrong with Sylvester's eyes? It looks like he has hay fever."

Randi doesn't look too concerned. "Probably got some dirt in them."

I head into the break room, where Shawn and Nick are watching a replay of Sylvester's race on the simulcast. The horses are running down the stretch.

"I hit the super on that one," Shawn says proudly. (For a superfecta, you pick the first four horses in correct order. Generally one makes more than one superfecta bet in order to hit it.) "Keyed Sylvester in with a bunch of others."

The replay of the fifth race starts playing.

"My sister bet on the four-horse," Nick says. "I tried to convince her otherwise, but she liked the name."

"Sucker bet," Shawn says.

I don't mention how I bet on the four-horse. Alex enters the break room, looking as he always does, crazed and amused.

"Did you bet 2–3–6 on the last race?" I ask him.

"Of course I did," he says. "It only paid $54.10, but those are my numbers. Like I told you, the key to it is consistency."

A WEEK AFTER sending Carole Serene a picture of Sylvester and a list of questions, I get a response from her by email. "I enjoyed

Sylvester very much; he has wonderful, gentle energy and wisdom, and a very cute nature," she writes to me. After Randi and I have time to "live with this information," she suggests that we arrange a follow-up communication.

The accompanying Word document reads like the transcript of an interview. The conversation starts with Carole asking Seth for permission to speak with Sylvester. Then it's Carole and Sylvester on the line:

CAROLE SERENE: Randi and Kevin have a great deal of affection for you and they want to be sure you are well and happy, so they have said it would be okay for you and me to talk so you can tell me if there's anything concerning you, or if you hurt anywhere, and how you feel generally about your life right now.

SYLVESTER: Oh I see, my goodness, this is a surprise for me. I'm just a horse here, so many horses here, and I didn't think I was special to anyone. Are we going to talk about me?

CAROLE SERENE: Yes, we are here to talk about you, only you. How do you feel about Randi?

SYLVESTER: Oh yes, Randi is good to me and we are friends. She takes good care of me and I have good food and she looks after my legs nicely.

CAROLE SERENE: Does she understand your mind too?

SYLVESTER: Oh yes, I think, she does know what is in my mind. Sometimes I am thinking something and she knows I am going to do it. She's quite smart you know.

Carole then asks Sylvester if he's disappointed when he loses a race:

SYLVESTER: Oh no, we take turns, you know. Some days we feel good and go faster than others and some days we hurt somewhere and can't, so we know that is how it will be. Some people here are disappointed sometimes, but I know I do my best always.

CAROLE SERENE: You used to get hormones before races, do you miss that?

SYLVESTER: What are hormones?

CAROLE SERENE: I believe it was something, maybe in your feed, that helped you to be stronger and run faster. Do you miss having that to help you run?

SYLVESTER: I don't know about that, I just eat and run and eat what I'm given...

Then Carole asks Sylvester how he feels about Blackie:

SYLVESTER: Oh, well, I do think that she is okay. Maybe not my favourite.

CAROLE SERENE: Does it bother you that she gets so much attention?

SYLVESTER: Well it shouldn't, no, but I like my time with Randi so much, well, you know, I am bad about this maybe. Well, I don't have to be silly about her attention to her, I know, because she likes me very much and I know it.

CAROLE SERENE: Well, you have just talked yourself out of jealousy haven't you? [Pause] Never mind, it's okay.

Later on in her transcript, Carole asks the question I'm dying to have answered:

CAROLE SERENE: Kevin has asked if you were upset when you were gelded and how has it changed your life?

SYLVESTER: Gelded?

CAROLE SERENE: Yes, castrated.

SYLVESTER: Oh that, well not very nice you know—not nice at

all and we did not like this at all and it hurt and I thought I had been a bad horse and was being punished. Was I?

CAROLE SERENE: No, Sylvester, not at all, you were not a bad horse.

It's surprising to me a horse would not understand the word "gelded," and yet know the word "castrated"—then again, is this the right moment to approach the situation logically? For a moment my skepticism builds, but then I get to the point in the transcript that concerns Sylvester's health. Carole hasn't met Sylvester, nor has she been given any information on his physical ailments outside of the questions about hormones.

CAROLE SERENE: How are your legs?

SYLVESTER: Oh, sometimes they are very good and other times, well, you know. I get swelling and soreness.

CAROLE SERENE: How are your eyes, Sylvester?

SYLVESTER: Why do you ask?

CAROLE SERENE: Not sure, I was just compelled to ask about your eyes, anything to tell me?

SYLVESTER: Well, they hurt sometimes.

CAROLE SERENE: What kind of hurt?

SYLVESTER: Kind of scratchy.

CAROLE SERENE: What does that look like for you, seeing funny?

SYLVESTER: Blurry a bit.

CAROLE SERENE: You know what, Randi will read this and if she doesn't already know, she will watch for this and take care of it for you.

SYLVESTER: Thank you.

⤳ 14 ⟜

~~SEE THE WORLD~~

C ELESTE AND I were in Louisville, Kentucky, when we started talking about our next trip. We left the breeding tour in time to catch the last few races that day at Churchill Downs, before spending the night at the Brown Hotel in Louisville. Under the hand-painted plaster-relief ceiling in its airy lobby lounge, we sampled a flight of bourbons in a high-backed love seat as teenagers on their prom night slipped into the hotel ballroom, which was shuddering with Top-Forty hits. We went back to our room, watched downloaded *30 Rock* episodes lying on my bed.

"Last night in Lexington, I was half-asleep and didn't know where I was," Celeste admitted in the dark, from her own bed. "I thought I heard something, so I got up and saw you standing over the toilet taking a leak."

"What's so funny?" I asked. "Didn't like what you saw?"

"It's been a while since I shared my space with anyone," she said. "I've missed it."

"Do you ever think about—" I started. "Never mind."

"What?"

"Do you ever think about what it would be like *if we did it?*"

"Yes."

"Really?"

"But I always thought it would ruin our friendship."

I groaned. "Before this week, I hadn't seen you in nine years. What kind of friendship is that?"

"True enough," she admitted, "but I'm still getting over my breakup."

"Well then, what are you doing later?" I asked. "Maybe in August?"

"I don't have anything planned this summer," she said, after mulling it over. "It's possible."

From this tepid reply, the wheels start grinding on another long-distance excursion. I decide this trip has to be racing-related so I can write it off; I also need an alibi to hang this trip on, lest my Kleenex-soft plans with Celeste fall through.

And, of course, they do. It's July, and we're on Skype. Celeste doesn't have a camera so I stare at a blank screen while she watches me eat buttered toast in a sleeveless undershirt.

"Um, sorry about my appearance," I say into my laptop. "It's hot out here."

"How dare you?" says the voice in fake outrage. "I'm wearing makeup to talk to you. I bought a new dress for our Skype session."

I smile. "And yet you can't get a webcam?"

"I actually put masking tape over it; there's only so much technology I can handle."

We trade quips until the issue of the trip comes up. "Are we still on for August?"

"You know, I don't think I can make it."

I'd braced for this; I half expected it. "Yeah, you're probably busy."

"Yeah," she says. "Plus, the guy I started dating and I are going to Ireland in the fall, and I can't really afford two trips."

I hadn't expected that. "Oh."

"Yeah, it just sort of happened. We've got a really intense physical connection, but he can be so antagonistic. Plus, he keeps a gun in the glove compartment of his car, which is pretty fucked up."

I realize that Celeste can see how crestfallen I look online; now I wish my own webcam was disabled. *"Oh."*

"I know you don't want to hear about it," she says. "I'm sorry."

"Then why do you tell me about it?"

"I don't have many people I can talk to."

Relating this exchange, I realize there's a version of it that's fairer to Celeste and less self-serving to me, a version that more forcefully portrays yours fondly as someone who can't take a hint, but I'm unable to offer it. Until that moment, there has been a corner of my heart reserved for her; after that conversation, it clears up. At least I'm grateful for that.

In front of my computer, I stare down at my to-do list with determination:

1. ~~BECOME A HOME OWNER~~ BOUGHT A RACEHORSE
2. ~~FIND TRUE LOVE~~ VISITED A BREEDING SHED
3. SETTLE DOWN & START A FAMILY
4. SEE THE WORLD
5. ~~LEARN ANOTHER LANGUAGE~~ TALKED LIKE A RAILBIRD
6. ~~START A RETIREMENT PLAN~~ REDUCED GAMBLING LOSSES
7. ~~GET A TATTOO~~ SERIOUSLY CONSIDERED GETTING A TATTOO

Looking back on my trip to Kentucky, I decide that maybe it wasn't about finding true love; maybe it was about seeing the world.

DESPITE THIS INEVITABLE disappointment, I can't escape feeling that I need to see more of that world. Except for my horse, there's nothing keeping me here this summer.

A week after my conversation with Celeste, I spend the evening browsing online for airfares and hotel deals while drinking Pimm's in Jamaican ginger ale with mint. It's about 3 AM when I finally go to bed. Out of habit, I've left my computer on, with the chat feature for my online profile still set on "available." When the chat program chirps awake, I consider letting this new message go unanswered. But I'm too curious about who might be saying hello this late. So I step back out of bed towards my desk.

LINDA LEE: Your late nights online will shorten your life.

KC: I will die of happiness. What are you doing up so early?

LINDA LEE: Coffee, yoga (I tried to fight it), then work.

KC: How long has it been since we last talked?

LINDA LEE: You mean, when was that supremely awkward goodbye? I dunno. I was waiting for you to make the first move.

KC: I'm not so forward nowadays. What have you been up to?

LINDA LEE: Being a librarian. Busy with work, personal bullshit.

KC: Personal BS = Your relationship status changed?

LINDA LEE: How nice of you to point that out.

KC: Moving on...

LINDA LEE: So, how about you? Are you up late trawling for a hookup?

KC: Uhh, actually, I was about to go to sleep.

LINDA LEE: I was reminded of you the other day.

KC: Good or bad?

LINDA LEE: Sort of good. Someone on the bus was complaining about a prize-winning book you hated. He sounded like you, too. Kinda funny, mostly whiney.

KC: Which book?

LINDA LEE: I forget now. I'll remember once we finish chatting.
KC: "Chatting."

One of the places I'd been thinking of visiting was the track in Saratoga Springs, New York, in time for the Travers Stakes. A side trip to Toronto wouldn't be too far out of the way, would it?

KC: It's funny you're messaging me now. I was going to contact you to say I will be in Toronto at the end of the month. Are you around?
LINDA LEE: Well, I live here...
KC: Okay, would you consent to see me?
LINDA LEE: Consent? You want me to donate a kidney?
KC: Drinks?
LINDA LEE: Uhhhhhhh, maybe not.
KC: Oh.
LINDA LEE: I'll be on a cleanse.
KC: Really? Until the end of the month?
LINDA LEE: I'm waiting until you get here to start it.

Maybe this trip won't be about seeing the world; maybe it'll be about finding true love. I guess I'm either a romantic or an idiot—probably both.

LINDA LEE AND I met while she was completing a library sciences degree. The first couple of times I saw her I forgot her name but knew she was the person I ran into everywhere I went. The impression she eventually made on me was that she was evasive; she said as little as possible without seeming either shy or above-it-all. This I found hard to resist, but then I came on too strong, was turned away, and was left to waddle to a shadowy corner of the room. Later on I saw her again with friends at a bar and we kept talking until there was nobody left.

My favourite memory of Linda Lee occurred a month after that, when we drove down to the Oregon coast and slept on the beach in only the duvet I snatched off my bed. While crossing the border, we'd bought fireworks from a roadside stand and tried to set them off that night, but the matches we had wouldn't light in the ocean breeze. A tall dude in dreadlocks appeared, like a shaman in Birkenstocks, from the swatch of hippies at the bonfire in the distance, handing us a log that was lit at one end. She took his torch and started lighting up our stash—the first bottle rocket shot out sideways towards the ocean. That was when I knew I had fallen hard for Linda Lee. She was a librarian with the heart of a shoplifting runaway.

When I was hanging around her, Linda Lee was still recovering from a broken engagement. I pretended I didn't care how she was half-present and fiercely independent. She liked me and didn't want to like me. It's funny, in an awful way, how another person's ambivalence firms up my own resolve: my heart sits on one end of a teeter-totter.

To make things worse, I was desperately trying to cram every possible bit of incident and chaos into my life to atone for my overly studious, incident-starved youth. I was behaving with the kind of reckless abandon I'd always valued in principle but could rarely muster myself. These were all conditions that allowed Linda Lee and me to accidentally conceive a child.

OVER THE NEXT month, I book my ticket and my rental vehicle, post-haste, and then get on a plane. We settle for breakfast at a diner near the house where I'm staying. She arrives at the booth still wearing her bike helmet, apologizing for her lateness as she shucks off the orange reflective vest that covers her wispy frame like a sandwich board. She's grown her hair out in the past two years, but then I know that from poring over her online photo albums. In fact, the first half-dozen things I ask her about, like her job, the well-being of her parents, her cat, even the knitting blog she used to maintain, all elicit answers I already possess and she likely knows I possess. But I ask them anyway, just to enter this information into our public record. She orders a western omelette, which she consumes head down, like she's reading a book.

"Why are you smiling?" she asks me.

I pick away at my pancakes, but there's no point brushing it off. She'll pester me until I tell her; so I tell her. "You always eat strangely," I say. "You treat breakfast like a mid-term."

Her eyes fall on me like thumbtacks into corkboard. "You used that line before," she says, the corners of her mouth turning down. "It was funnier the first time."

"Sorry, I'm out of practice."

She eats like that to avoid eye contact, the same reason she draws on coasters at bars and knits mittens on streetcars. But today she's also eating quickly because she's in a hurry. When she's done, she apologizes again for having to leave to run an off-day errand. As kiss-offs go, it could be worse. At her insistence, we split the bill. Outside on the sidewalk, I watch her unlock her bike.

"This wasn't as bad as I thought it would be," she says. "How long are you here for?"

"I've got plans tonight," I say, "and Thursday."

"What are you doing tomorrow?"

"I was planning to go to the track," I say. "No one wants to go with me."

"Woodbine?" she asks me, buckling her helmet strap.

"Yeah," I admit reluctantly, "but we could go somewhere else."

"No, I'm cool with that," she says before pushing off into traffic. "Text me the details."

THE NEXT EVENING, when I arrive in my rental car, Linda Lee is waiting for me outside of her apartment in the Roncesvalles neighbourhood. "I knew it would be you when I saw the car pull up two feet from the curb," she says, stepping into the car. "You're even wishy-washy about parking." It's the last week of August, and it's not quite warm enough to wear a track-appropriate frock, but she has on a wide-brimmed hat and a string of pearls as well as her T-shirt, cardigan, and jeans.

"You know what I'm excited about?" she asks me as we pull away. "Gambling."

I nod rabidly. "I've gone five days without a bet."

"I was in Atlantic City last year before my sister's stagette and won $1,200 on the slots," she says. "It was better than falling in love. Have you gotten any better at playing the ponies?"

"Marginally," I say, wincing at her reference to our last trip to a racecourse.

"And did you bring a map?" she says. "I don't know how to get to Woodbine."

I point to the GPS mounted on the air vent. "We've got this. I bought it last year when I almost drove into a ditch heading to a wedding in the suburbs while trying to read the Google Maps printout on the steering wheel." In its stern, Midwest-American female voice, the GPS directs me onto the Gardiner Expressway. "Now I have no trouble getting to weddings, but this thing's not much of a date."

She points at the machine. "She's *bossy*. How do you put up with her?"

She groans as we ascend the expressway on-ramp and find our place in the late rush-hour traffic. "When are you going to New York?" she asks me.

I already mentioned that I was leaving two days from now. "Friday."

"Who are you bringing with you?" she asks, and I sense an opening for an invitation.

"No one," I tell her. In fact, the idea of driving alone for twelve hours straight terrifies me. "What are your plans this weekend?"

She hesitates. "There are a couple of things."

"Can you get out of them?" I ask.

"Maybe."

"When was the last time you went on a last-second road trip?" I ask her.

"I don't care to say."

From the highway, we see the track, a glass and concrete structure painted the same kind of industrial, mustard colour that you'd see on a suburban entertainment complex with auditorium seating and food courts.

The original Woodbine was in the east end of the city, launched in 1874 by a local businessman, Joseph Duggan, who named it after a pub he once owned. New Woodbine Racetrack opened in 1956 and was the location of Secretariat's last race in 1973 and a Breeders' Cup in 1996; it still hosts the Queen's Plate, the oldest continuously run stakes in North America.

Inside, I squeal at the sight of the three different racing ovals that make up the track. There's an inside dirt track that runs seven-eighths of a mile for harness racing, then a mile-long synthetic racing oval, one of only nine artificial surfaces in North America for thoroughbreds. The outermost track, the E.P. Taylor turf course, is a mile and a half long—a gargantuan length for North American racing. It acquired its name from the tycoon who not only founded the Jockey Club of Canada, but also owned Northern Dancer.

"Northern Dancer," I tell Linda Lee, "was not only, indisputably, the greatest horse ever bred in Canada but is generally considered the twentieth century's most important sire."

Linda Lee smiles. "You sound like a boy talking about dinosaurs."

Born in Oshawa, the runty, dark bay winner of the Canadian Triple Crown, the Kentucky Derby, and the Preakness in 1964 not only fathered champions on dirt and grass around the world, but had babies and grandbabies who've become prominent sires in their own right. By the mid-eighties, his stud fee was $1 million without even the guarantee of a live foal.

Like other great Canadians who emigrated to fully realize their celebrity, from Celine Dion to Michael Ignatieff, "Canada's Horse" was shipped to Maryland, to be closer to potential broodmares, in 1969. According to Peter Gzowski's racetrack memoir, *An Unbroken Line*, Taylor brought Northern Dancer to Woodbine for one last trot around the oval before his admiring fans.

"In the van on the way over," Gzowski wrote, "Northern Dancer must have thought he was being taken to the breeding shed, for he came down the ramp with an ambitious and generous erection, and before [trainer and exercise rider] Pete McCann had him saddled, he took him behind a willow tree and, to distract him, slapped him heartily on the nose."

We arrive just after the second race. For much of the third one, we're in line for beer and rib sandwiches, which leaves us mere minutes to pick our winners.

I'm trying to carry on with my good betting habits and place a conservative $10 win-show bet on the second favourite, Venganza, in the third race, a mile-long turf race.

Linda Lee steps up to the window next to me. She places a win bet on Venganza, the one-horse, but also wants to make an exactor bet (i.e., one that picks the first two horses to finish the race, in their exact order—also known as an exacta) on Venganza with the other horse she likes, the race favourite. "What number is Captive Spirit?" she asks me.

I flip through my copy of the *Form* and see Captive Spirit as the race analyst's pick to place. "Two," I say mistakenly.

We settle into one of the folding blue bleacher seats overlooking the eight pole. As the horses lope towards the gate, I look around the grandstand. It's a half-full, half-interested crowd. Some of them still wear the pastels of July; the others are already in the earth tones of autumn. Those in shorts and

T-shirts wear them with an almost joyless defiance, and many of them tie sweaters and jacket sleeves around their waists. They all look like they'll be teetotalling or nursing a beer for the whole evening, wary of a Thursday morning hangover at work.

"Do you remember the last time we were at the track?" Linda Lee asks me.

"How can I forget?" I say. "That wasn't much fun."

"I'm surprised we're here," she says. "You really pick your spots."

"I was hoping you wouldn't point that out."

"You know I can't resist pointing things out."

We visited Hastings Park a week before her appointment to end her pregnancy. The part of me that wanted to enact my own unlived life was heartbroken. By then, we had begun to half hate each other. We headed to the track, which she had never before visited, for some kind of novel distraction. I drank six plastic cups of draught beer and felt sick. Linda Lee disappeared for half an hour to call her sister.

I remember betting poorly that afternoon—on anything, for no reason—mainly because I felt I was owed some good luck. In psychological terminology, that feeling I had is known as "gambler's fallacy." There have been moments this year when I've wondered whether my own recent engagement with the track hasn't been, in fact, an attempt at recapturing and mastering that situation. If I could be a handicapping genius, then that personal catastrophe—a nipple-twister for the ages—would be conquered.

Within two weeks of our trip to the track, I left to attend an artist's residency in a lighthouse on the east coast. When I returned, Linda had graduated and gone back to Toronto.

Back at Woodbine, the race begins and Venganza wins by three lengths from inside, but the real excitement for us comes when the two-horse, Spend Now and Save, prevails to place. Captive Spirit is actually running in the nine hole, but my error gave Linda Lee the winner.

"You got lucky," she says to me.

"So did you," I say.

We stay longer, but being at the track, and the memory it inspires, has made us both quiet and morose. It's a relief when Linda Lee suggests we leave. In the car, without any prompting, she mentions an unbreakable lunch date she has scheduled with her mother on Saturday. We sit in silence waiting for the voice of the GPS—smug, almost scolding—to tell us we've arrived at our destination.

PASSING THROUGH UPSTATE New York, I drive on two-lane highways that cut through wooded hills, towns with brick-lined Main Streets, and past apocalyptic biblical quotations hand-painted on billboards, to Saratoga Springs, a town that's stuffed with Victorian homes and is equally famous for its mineral baths and its track.

With its gazebo-style entrance, red-and-white striped tented awnings, vendors hawking lemonade, pretzels, and oil paintings of Barbaro and Rachel Alexandra, the track nicknamed "the Spa" retains the genteel fairground atmosphere of its first meet in 1863. For five weeks between late July and Labor Day, over twenty thousand visitors come each day not only to see New York's finest thoroughbreds race, but also to enjoy the track itself. Although the clouds are heavy when I arrive late Friday afternoon, it still feels summery here.

The Saratoga crowd is dressed in seersucker suits, summer frocks, and hats. Their multitudes make it hard to find a seat. The grandstands at the Spa, under spiky cupolas, are only half-full, but you have to pay to sit there, and even spots on the benches inside facing the betting windows and television screens are, if not occupied, then informally reserved with newspapers or a baseball cap. I flatten out my *Form* on a trash can facing a hot-dog vendor while I make a bet, trying to factor in performances on turf versus those on artificial surfaces.

It does me no good. By the last race, I've lost $40, and I nurse two beers at a nearby bar as the traffic clears. Then I head out to find my accommodations. The hotels in Saratoga charge double their normal rates during the meet, and judging by the number of "NO VACANCY" signs I see, they could probably gouge deeper. It's for value and quaintness that I'm staying at the Triple Crown Motel, two highway exits down from the track. Across from a jockey's dummy with a ceramic Secretariat, the motel sign proudly advertises its "color TVs by RCA." I wait fifteen minutes for the front-desk clerk, who's stepped out, to return with her tallboy in a brown paper bag and check me in.

Each room is named for a different Triple Crown winner. Room number seven, the Assault room, smells like someone's aged grandmother, bearing the traces of both conscientious cleaning and un-concealable decay. I settle into the lumpy double bed with the TV replaying the day's races and start making my picks for the biggest day on the Saratoga calendar, Travers Day.

The race day is highlighted by the Travers Stakes, the oldest stakes competition in the U.S. Along with the Breeders' Cup in November, it's one of the biggest race cards in the back half of the year. Like the Triple Crown races in the spring, the "Midsummer Derby" has its own mythology. Jim Dandy, a 100-to-1 shot, beat Triple Crown winner Gallant Fox at the 1930 Travers, which also feeds Saratoga's reputation as the "Graveyard of the Favourites." After all, it's here that Secretariat, shortly after knocking off the Triple Crown in 1973, lost to a chestnut gelding named Onion, and Man o' War lost his only race, to Upset, in 1919.

When I arrive after the first race at 11:35 AM, the nine-fur-long dirt track has turned to mud. I had planned my entire trip around the possibility that all three Triple Crown winners— Mine That Bird, Rachel Alexandra, and Summer Bird—would be running at the Travers. Summer Bird is here, but his half-brother, Mine That Bird, was scratched a few days ago to recover from minor surgery. Rachel Alexandra, the super filly who beat both the boys this year in separate races, is kept out by trainer Steve Rasmussen to run in the Woodward Stakes, held here the next week.

The race begins. The horses bobble, en masse, as they tear into the mud. At various points, as the horses speed along the backstretch, the numbers on my tickets pulse to life. But then Summer Bird gains the lead and builds on it; Quality Road, the Florida Derby winner, falls back from contention enough to let Hold Me Back make a late charge for second. I get the top four horses, but not all on the same ticket.

Stepping out onto the apron on my way to the exit, I mill with the crowd that's gathered around the winning horse. Where I come from, no horse qualifies as a celebrity. Here, though, people swarm the Belmont and Travers champion not only to peruse the horse, but to take part in his veneration. Kent Desormeaux, Summer Bird's mud-encrusted jock, waves back to the crowd as his horse puffs.

Other Travers Day attendees begin dispersing to the lots and backyards they've paid to park in. I consider leaving, but realize there's no rush to get to Manhattan—my next stop. Driving alone has been, as expected, a miserable, clock-watching experience. I'm seeing the world, I guess, but doing it solo. Lingering in the mob, I aim my crappy digital camera at the champion thoroughbred, but only get the tops of other people's heads.

⋙ 15 ⋘

AUCTION DAY, PART ONE

LESSON THREE: Never Settle for What You've Earned.

While horseracing was in a shabby state, it still brought me into daily contact with those who were better off than I. The racetrack confirmed my belief that there was no positive correlation between industriousness and material prosperity. Randi worked two jobs, but deadbeat owners and gimpy thoroughbreds regularly put her behind on her own bills. Meanwhile, Hastings was a sandbox for people whose fortunes were derived long ago, and who transferred their competitive urges onto their horses—equine athletes that generally raced several notches above my own. The intrinsic value of my own efforts wasn't recognized.

After resisting it for many years, I succumbed to the idea that life had its winners and losers, the prom queens and book-club members, the quarterbacks and the writing-workshop leaders, and the only reason to cry out against injustice was if it gave you an opening to pummel some groin.

Being a professional sports owner was grand, but I wanted to be vaulted into the winner's circle of life. I wanted to be an overlord and not a vassal; the man behind the curtain and not the puppet with a hand in its rear. I pictured myself sitting impassively in an owner's box, in a charcoal-grey suit and a camel-hair coat, chewing on the knob of my antique walking stick, unlit Cohiba in my fish stick-cold fingers, surrounded by my second wife; the children from my previous marriage; and the grandchildren from my children's previous marriages. I wanted to make decisions and eat free popcorn.

I returned from my trip to the east coast ornery and dissatisfied. Summer was ending. I deserved a finer life.

FROM *WHAT I LEARNED AT THE TRACK:*
A Manual of Failure

FOR BLACKIE'S SIXTH race of the season, I rent a box seat with a view overlooking the eight pole. My friends and I might not get our own little TV screen to watch the simulcast the way we would in the boxes closer to the finish line—the ones people buy for the season—but waitresses come and take our orders for beer, and, for only $15, that small luxury makes me forget my owner inadequacy.

In the *Form,* I notice contenders from Blackie's last race; an overwhelming amount of the money is going to a horse named Kokeeno, a six-year-old chestnut mare who's dropping a class. Blackie nuzzles the pony as she's led down the post parade. It's a ten-horse field and she's at her longest odds this year, 10-to-1, to win. The owners of the horses in the race are announced, and I stand up and wave to the disinterested crowd as my name is called.

With under a minute to post, I find Randi taking her spot at the picnic table facing the top of the lane.

"How did the Girl do?" I ask. Another one of Randi's horses, Aubrey Road, ran in the first race, but I didn't want to get to the track too early, lest I lose more money.

"Second," she says. "That's how it goes when you have no fucking luck."

(At the time, I don't know that the day after Randi claimed the horse she couldn't even walk her. Randi turned her out to the farm for a month, Alex brought ice over on his bike for her legs—it was hours and hours of work just so she could enter the race. In this sprint, the horse is put in a ridiculous pace and is beaten by a horse that won five times.)

You don't often hear trainers or owners talk about luck actually going their way, how their horse might have profited from another's horse's misfortune, but any bad luck they experience becomes embroidered into their own ill-starred life story, and the length of the race, from the opening gate to the finish line, is rife with opportunities for a personal persecution narrative— be it a common stumble leaving the gate or some extraordinary hex—like one trainer in Randi's shed row whose horse led on the back turn until he hit a bird that had swooped down into his path. The horse was so rattled by the encounter that he allowed another horse to pass him for the win.

I have no time to commiserate before the race starts. Blackie starts well, coming out to an early lead.

"Don't do that!" Randi yells at her horse.

Blackie settles down on her own, moving behind Kokeeno and Notis Me, who finished ahead of her in the previous race, before drawing back to them midway through the backstretch. At the far turn, when the horses look like ten stooges trying to funnel into the same doorway, she takes the lead. Randi, who's not usually demonstrative when her horses race, steps towards the track and starts pumping her fist as she cheers Blackie on. Blackie should be pouring it on, but she just sits there.

We later learn that the rider, Perez, dropped his stick at the top of the stretch. Without the stick to "call on her for her best," he tries to egg Blackie on by scrubbing against her neck with his hands, but she doesn't understand this improvised cue. The two-horse, Flower Hill, and the four-horse, Quickens, pass her. Randi bolts towards the racing oval, screaming about the rider, even before the photo finish reveals that Blackie managed to hang onto third.

I happen to make $100 on my show bet, but I'm indifferent. For the first time this season, the race result doesn't faze me. The horse could have won, she could have finished dead last. A sense of dissatisfaction sits in my chest like a throw pillow as I realize that my horse will never be one of the legends I've spent the summer reading about, not even a local hero whose soaring finishes and heart-wrenching close calls build up to a cathartic triumph. For a claiming horse, race one in the season is not much different from race six except for the changing seasons and extra mileage on your depreciating asset. Owning Blackie will not change my life. This is as good as it gets—for the horse and for me.

MY INTEREST IN owning a future equine legend leads me to the yearling sale, which is held in an airy barn at an equestrian park in Langley. Like most people here, I've come not only to gawk at the gawky colts and fillies but also to watch more prosperous folks blow their fortunes.

The horses auctioned today could end up never running, but they have the potential to become stakes calibre and win prestigious local races. Several years back, the eventual winner of the 2003 B.C. Derby, the biggest event in the local racing calendar, Roscoe Pito, was purchased here for only $2,993 by a group that included a bartender at Hastings; the lifetime earnings of the horse, who ended up racing in California, were $608,277. Unlike a claiming horse, a young horse purchased here won't run until the following spring, if training goes well, and only in a handful of races as a two-year-old, if at all. In that time, you will be paying for its training and upkeep with no money coming in. If horseracing is a slow poison, then buying a yearling is cyanide.

The hamstrung economy doesn't bode well for the auction. A recent sale in Alberta saw sales drop forty-five percent.

Local breeders, whose horses are eligible for B.C.-bred bonuses and special stakes races, are likely selling at a loss. The horses, with numbered tags on their hips, are led onto a stage that has been decorated with leafy houseplants. Behind them in a desk, Mike Heads, the Hastings simulcast commentator, talks up a horse's pedigree.

"Number eleven, property of Susi Schaer, Canmor Farms, agent, is the filly by the mare Flirtatious Wonder," Heads says. "Flirtatious Wonder is a stakes winner of over $200,000. She's the half-sister to Raise the Rent and In Gold We Trust. She's had three foals to the races, two of them winners, $34,000 in earnings."

As the horses are brought onto the stage and circled around, an auctioneer calls prices in a musical gargle:

"Awww, diggiddydown, diggiddydown, diggiddydown, dig-giddydown, three thousand. *Aww, diggiddydo, diggiddydo, diggiddydo, diggiddydo, diggiddydo, diggiddydo,* two thousand."

Standing in front of the stage are a number of assistants, dressed in the cowboy equivalent of business casual—suit jackets and ties with Stetsons and boots. When someone nods or raises a hand to bid, they pump their fists and yell, "YEEE-AAAAHHHHHH!" Occasionally, a horse will whinny in response. Even though I have no stake in the bidding, my heart pulses with joy every time one of these assistants offers this celebratory, encouraging scream. I suppose that's why it's done.

The auctioneer goes down to a thousand before eventually selling the horse for $1,100.

Most of the bidders are seated in folding chairs within sight of the auctioneer and his assistants. Horatio Kemeny of Swift Thoroughbreds sits in the front row for most of the afternoon. He and his partner Mark Mache disappear to get lunch outside. After they finish eating, I meet up with him on his way back to his chair. In a dark shirt and blazer, Kemeny has light brown hair, a neatly trimmed beard, and a sturdy build. Mache is tall like an NBA power forward, but, with his shoulder-length blond hair, has an amiable, youthful aura. So far, they've purchased three horses for $6,500, $20,000, and $19,000.

"One of them was good value," he says, trying to catch the attention of Mache without accidentally bidding. "The other two were fair value."

I've largely avoided interactions with other owners this season, rationalizing to myself that they are normally alpha-male business types with no time for my low-earning ilk. And, if I did speak to them, they'd be so guarded to the point of brain-gouging dullness. Some racetrackers I've talked to back me up on that count, suggesting that the entrepreneurs and executives who get into the sport do so to acquire a contained burst of the unpredictability, zest, and eccentricity that they've so fastidiously squelched from every other corner of their life. But in absolute honesty, I've avoided meeting other owners because they call to attention my huge wannabe status as someone who might be able to impress friends with his four-figure investment for part of a bottom claimer, but is only an owner in the loosest definition.

The Swift Thoroughbreds guys definitely incite these intimations of poseurdom. While both of them are only forty, Kemeny and Mache's attachment to the sport began in the early 1980s when Mache's grandmother brought them to the track for the first time as twelve-year-olds. The two friends would ride across town on their bikes to the track, recruiting desperate horseplayers to place bets for them using money they collected from bottle deposits.

"The place was hopping back then," Kemeny says. "There was racing on five days, the handle was a million dollars a day. Now I don't think it's more than $200,000. It was the only game in town. The truth was that you came here on a Welfare Wednesday"—the day of the month when welfare cheques arrived—"and you couldn't move. Everybody wanted to be here."

Later on, the two friends would team up to form MindSpan, a video game company that created the baseball video game HardBall. After they sold their business in 2002, they got into horses. Swift Thoroughbreds has forty-four horses listed on its website, each horse costing about $20,000 to maintain.

Kemeny and Mache not only employ an entire stable, but also bring in new horses that get absorbed into the pool of horses that change hands at the track. A couple of years back, they also belonged to the group of owners who helped restore the purses after a cut by track management. Maybe in other parts of the world racehorses remain fashionable instruments for flaunting wealth, but in this city and other places where the track's lustre has been worn down to its grimy base, the Swift guys are eccentric benefactors of a precariously unpopular cultural institution, like chamber music or metered verse. According to backstretch gossip, the annual budget for their stable is $3 million—a sum that their annual winnings don't come within fifteen lengths of matching.

Kemeny estimates that maybe half the horses he buys at the sale end up racing. "The other half we sell for cheap, find them good homes," he says. Swift Thoroughbreds's trainer, Dino Condilenios, comes the day before for the parade to look at the horses and, with Mache and Kemeny, compiles A and B lists. "Conformation is at least as important as pedigree."

Pleasantly surprised by the turnout and the prices the horses are going for, Kemeny, who says he's allergic to horses, excuses himself as he returns to his seat to bid on the next entry. "I don't think he'll come cheap," he says, before returning to his spot. Kemeny keeps the assistants screaming as the horse goes for $42,000. At the end of the day, Swift spends $216,500 on ten horses.

Beyond the bidders in the folding chairs, on portable bleacher seats and in a beer garden to the side, are onlookers—trainers and jockeys and grooms who just want to be part of the fun. Compared with the auctions at Keeneland and Saratoga, where horses have been purchased for eight-figure sums, the amounts spent here are a trifle—barely enough to fill a briefcase with twenties. For most other people, these prices still equal their life savings or the equity in their homes, all of it kissed away with a nod to the auctioneer. Here, for now, everyone's spent his money wisely.

AT THE AUCTION, I hear my name called and see Kulwant behind the beer garden gates. "Pick up any champion horse-flesh?" he asks me.

"Just window-shopping," I say, leaning over the fence. "What brings you here?"

He shrugs, rolling the bottom rim of his empty plastic cup of beer against his table. "I had some friends driving out here, so I tagged along," he says. "This is cheap fun. At least for me."

Kulwant lets me buy him another beer. Work ended for him a few hours earlier, and maybe it's his fatigue and the beer, but his fangs are temporarily retracted. He even shows me a printout for a van that he's saving his money to buy, as though it were his own yearling. We talk about sports and books and movies.

It's in this hospitable conversational space that I allow myself to become philosophical.

"Do you ever wonder how much you'd be worth in an auction?" I ask him. "And whether you'd be worth your price?"

"A slave auction? Or the kind where you buy a date for charity?" he replies. "'No' to both."

"Say these horses are like newly minted holders of bachelor's degrees," I continue. "Some of them come from good families, others have good grades, or display talent in their classes, and you bid high on the ones you thought would be the winners and avoided the ones with the weak knees. Do you think you'd live up to your potential? Would you have exceeded it?"

"Jesus, why do you always measure yourself against others?" he asks me. "Why can't you be happy with all the cashmere sweaters you already own?"

"I'm just making an analogy—"

"It's a *bad* analogy. If you or I don't live up to expectations, old friends stop returning phone calls. That's all that happens—no big loss." He looks over to a chestnut mare being circled onstage. "You don't want to know what happens to these horses when they can't run."

"I don't return your calls because I can't stand your bitterness," I say. "You resent anyone who has even an inkling of success. You shit on them for wanting more."

The scowl collects on Kulwant's face like dust. He finishes his beer and gets up.

MY NEXT TRIP to Hastings comes when I attempt to introduce Randi to Carole Serene. Randi finds the animal communicator's transcript amusing, but won't believe that I didn't tell Carole about Sylvester's eyes. (The redness in his eyes after that race had long cleared away.) Still, she agrees right away to see her. "This is going to be hilarious," she says.

Carole is en route from a meeting with the agent responsible for renting out her vintage Jaguar for movie shoots. We meet in the parking lot by the horseman's entrance and, with my hot walker's licence, I sign her into the backstretch.

"How do you feel among these animals?" I ask her as we move into sight of Barn A.

"I feel at home," says Carole, who's wearing a pink blouse and white slacks and open-toed slippers. She smiles at the horses in the barns with stalls facing outside. "I haven't tuned into any of them, if that's what you're asking."

Yeah, that was what I was asking.

"It's quite a breakthrough that Randi is willing to meet with me," she tells me, sidestepping a pile of fresh horse dung.

"Well, I wouldn't call it a breakthrough," I say.

"I'm under no illusion that Randi believes anything I do, but I would like her to give credibility to what I was told by Sylvester so that we can help him towards wellness."

When we get into the stable, Randi is not to be seen, so I introduce her to Sylvester. She approaches him, placing her hand on his neck. "Hi, sweetheart," she says. "It's me, Carole Serene. Remember? How are you feeling?"

"What's it like seeing the animal you've communicated with?" I ask her, as I look in the feed closet for a carrot that Carole can offer her friend.

"I love to see the recognition in their eyes," she says. "And suddenly, now we have relaxation. Do you see that change?"

"Well," I say, "his ears are all pricked up."

Carole keeps her hand on the side of Sylvester's face. Normally, at the sight of visitors, he'll act like he's front row at a Motörhead concert, but he watches Carole calmly.

"You want to talk some more, dear?" she says to him. "We can do that."

As we wait for Randi, I ask Carole to explain a puzzling detail in her transcript—why Sylvester would understand the word "castrate," but not "geld."

"That's a good question," Carole says. "I think it's a matter of what the horses hear around the stable. 'Geld' is more of a polite term. Usually, they use the word 'cut' in the stables."

"So animals have vocabularies?" I ask.

"Yes, what they hear around them. Dogs have very good vocabularies, though not so much cats."

"Why's that?"

"Dogs have families, while cats have staff," she tells me. "They don't pay attention."

"Do you think you could ask Sylvester for any betting tips?"

Carole thinks about it for a moment. "I was surprised by what Sylvester told me about how the horses know who'll win," she says.

"So, the horses fix the races?" I ask.

"I wouldn't say that. But they know who's feeling good. So, if I were so inclined, I could actually ask Sylvester who he thinks will do good in the race."

"Really?"

"Your eyes just lit up."

"I imagine they did."

Randi returns from lunch, in her puffy vest and jeans, followed by Aki, her part-time groom. I realize soon after introductions are made that I've put everyone in an awkward position. Randi, while curious to meet Carole Serene, doesn't accept advice from anyone, much less an animal communicator. Carole, on the other hand, isn't used to dealing with skeptical clients. What I've ended up doing, in an unintentional but utterly careless way, is challenge the abilities of both of them.

"Blackie has the most adorable personality," Carole says in Randi's break room. "She's very sweet, isn't she?"

Randi slumps back on the couch, and then sucks back her cigarette. "No, she's not that nice."

"She'll try to kick you," Aki adds. At twenty-two, she is a brainy, aspiring vet doing a double major in English and biology.

"I didn't think you guys were coming this afternoon," Randi says to me. "I thought you guys were coming for the Friday night race."

"I can't go to the races," Carole admits. "I'm too sensitive, I guess. When they're stressed, I'm stressed."

One half of Randi's face drops as though she's been personally attacked. "If you counted all the races in the world that run, it's probably a very minute fraction of bad that goes on," she says. "It just looks horrendous."

"I just can't cope."

"It's no more common than a guy walking across the street and getting hit by a bus. I love all my animals. I try my hardest not to put them in that situation, but shit happens. I broke down only one horse in thirty years and I hope to keep it that way."

Carole nods. "I know."

"They break their legs out in the field. You think you're doing them a favour and they run against the fence and break a shoulder."

"They get in a fight," Aki adds. "They get kicked in the face."

Carole tries to calm Randi down. "Your horses are so protected here," she says. "They're conditioned."

"But still, anything can happen."

I try to change the subject, but I pick the wrong one when I mention Sylvester's possible retirement. Earlier this week, Aki mentioned to me that Randi was thinking about turning Sylvester into a show horse.

"Why is everyone so interested in what I'm going to do with Sylvester?" she asks. "I'm not going to kill him."

Carole needs to make another appointment, so we step back out to the shed row, where Aki introduces us to the new horses that a Seattle trainer has sent Randi to race at Hastings. Carole turns back to Sylvester one last time, imparting her farewells to him with a hand on his head.

Randi glares at us, and then looks to her favourite horse. "They giving you a hard time, Sylvester?" she says. "They don't know you won a hundred grand. Not a lot of horses can say that."

⤳ 16 ⤶

AUCTION DAY, PART TWO

LESSON FIVE: Fail to Appreciate Your Horse.

Until the year I became an owner, I felt I was a connoisseur of under-appreciation. My abilities, attributes, and contributions had been routinely overlooked; accolades had been given to people with shinier hair who wrote their own Wikipedia entries.

And yet I was also a chronic under-appreciator in my own right.

The indisputable fact that people who think horseracing equals animal cruelty were fools didn't preclude me from being an indisputably massive fool myself...

FROM *WHAT I LEARNED AT THE TRACK:*
A Manual of Failure

WHEN I FIND out that Blackie is racing in the second race that Saturday, I am irrationally exuberant about her chances. She's running in a six-horse field, back at a $5,000 claiming price. And, according to my freshly purchased copy of the *Form,* she has the highest Beyer Speed

Figure of all the horses in their most recent races. After almost winning without a stick on her in a ten-horse field, she ought to knee-cap her competition today.

An hour before the gates discharge, Randi warns me that the race is evenly matched, and that several of the horses in the race like to run up front like Blackie, which is why Sultry Eyes, who's beaten and been beaten by my horse, is a favourite. I treat her pessimism as verbal static and spend the afternoon with my ears pricked as though a victory is predestined.

With half a dozen friends, I watch Blackie saunter down the post parade, looking sharp as she nudges against the pony. "So, when Blackie wins," I tell my friends, "I want you guys to come down with me for the photo."

Everyone's placed money on Blackie, and I put down $130 of my own and other people's money.

With Perez on her again, Blackie breaks out well from the five-hole, rushing to the front of the pack before settling for third at the clubhouse turn behind two other frontrunners, Grayross Gal and Archery. The first quarter comes at 22.19, which, I realize later, is too fast for her. Perez makes his move midway through the backstretch, loosening his hold on the horse. Blackie moves to second at the turn, then at the top of the lane, where she runs fifth from the rail. All the horses are closely bunched together.

With the horses coming into view, my friends and I get up to scream for Mocha Time by her stable nickname. Others around us, with their plastic cups of beer held to their chests like nursing infants, yell out the numbers they picked with tender, albeit impersonal, coaxing: *Come on, two... you can do it, two! Don't give up ground... come on, two!* The ones cheering on their exotic wagering picks sound even odder, like orgasmic safe-crackers: *"One-four-seven! One-four-seven! Yes... yes... yes!"*

Even though we're screaming on a first-name basis, it doesn't help. Blackie has used up her burst of speed. Beautiful Breeze comes in through the inside and takes the lead, while Sultry Eyes, the rater, also advances past her. According to summary results, Blackie finished fifth by three lengths. It's her worst performance this season.

Having talked up the horse's chances, I apologize to my friends who lost money. "I accept full responsibility," I say, in my blazer with sunglasses on my forehead, "which doesn't mean I'll reimburse you."

"It's all right," one friend tells me.

I drain a beer, then another one. Down $130 for the day, I start betting wildly, placing $20 on a long shot to win, then another $20 on the favourite. Both lose. Things don't improve when I run into a friend who struts by us after hitting a $2 triactor for $150. His other friend has a $6 box on that same bet.

It's not as though I'm fully out of control, but I'm not my usual thrifty self. I'm like the shy, quiet co-worker who starts dancing with his shirt off at the club and ends the night trying to trade his laptop for cocaine. Or the garrulous optimist whose eyes go dead after four glasses of whisky.

"Hey, we want to see the horse," a friend says.

I push my face farther into my copy of the *Form*. "Sure, sure," I tell her, "after the next race."

"I don't care if you're hungry," another friend jokes, adopting an angry authoritarian's voice. *"We're not eating until Daddy wins his money back."*

"Okay, fine, let's go."

In the stables, as Blackie is being walked, my friends feed apples to Randi's other horses. I approach Randi, who isn't as unhappy about the race as she had been the last time, when Perez dropped the stick.

"What happened?" I ask her outside the feed room.

"We just didn't get any luck," she says with a fatalistic flatness as she fills up buckets of feed. "She was five wide at the turn."

"I mean, did Perez do something again?" I ask insistently.

"Nope," Randi says.

Her voice rises in irritation. I shouldn't be testing her temper but the dropped stick from the previous race emboldens me. "Is it because she had too long of a layoff?" I ask. "What went wrong?"

"I wish you'd quit fucking thinking there's something wrong," she says, carrying out one of the buckets to one of her new horses, Rooster. "You always think she did something wrong."

"I don't mean in that way..." I say.

"The fucking thing tries her little heart out."

"Then why didn't she win?" I blurt.

Rooster backs into the stall as Randi dumps his dinner into his tub. Alex returns Blackie to her stall, and my friends become preoccupied with petting and photographing her.

Blackie, I am fairly certain, loves having her photo taken. At the sound of a lens focusing automatically, she preens and makes faces. Her ears prick and her nostrils flare, she tosses her forelock over her eyes and bares her big buckteeth.

I glare at my mare, thinking to myself that she doesn't deserve the attention. *It's only because of me that anyone is making a fuss over you.* But the horse doesn't seem fazed by my sour mood. As Blackie continues to ignore me, Randi steps in front of me.

"In all my fucking life," she tells me, "I've never had to deal with such trouble from some guy who don't know fuck-all about horses and horseracing, and only has ten percent of a horse."

"I've got more than that now," I remind her. "I wrote another cheque."

"Don't worry, I haven't forgotten," she says, disappearing back into the feed room to prepare Blackie's dinner. "You just don't get it."

FOR DAYS AFTERWARDS, I sulk over Blackie's poor performance and avoid anything that reminds me of my humiliation.

Out of a need for distraction, I finally attend to long-delayed errands, which include retrieving three heavy boxes' worth of paper from my parents' house. I don't have enough space in my apartment to keep this material, which means slowly weeding out the essentials. Most of it I relinquish easily: copies of guitar magazines and old English essays.

A few items, though, invite tricky feelings. This includes a cache of letters and postcards that Kulwant sent me a decade ago. In the early days of email, Kulwant held out from electronic correspondence longer than most. The notes come from around the world, his cramped, neat scrawl filling out pages and postcards.

Reading through his messages, I remember how funny he could be—he would whiteout the dialogue bubbles in *Peanuts* strips and write in references to hand jobs and gonorrhea—how his own strident view of the world encased a precise and idealistic sense of purpose.

A surprising number of his letters were encouraging. Before I became the self-satisfied person Kulwant likes to ridicule, I was the insecure, needy person he coddled and hectored positively. Sifting through a batch of letters that Kulwant wrote to me when I first moved away to grad school, I reread his attempts to cajole me into good spirits with a walking tour of fictional landmarks near my student apartment (e.g., I lived three blocks from Dylan Thomas's falconer and across town from Miles Davis's favourite yogourt stand), and, later, the patient critiques he offered on my novel-in-progress, which he hated but still helped improve. In all these letters, the parts I loved about him co-mingled and overlapped with his most obnoxious and self-inflating qualities.

On Kulwant's meticulously updated website, I find a listing for a performance in a converted east side deli. I bring with me a friend, Antonia, a live-music blogger working on her dissertation in art history. The place is crowded with hollow-eyed beardos and women with chopped bangs and plastic-rimmed glasses that stand out on their pale faces. We take a space behind the deli counter, which is crammed blindly with CDs, cans of cheap lager, and a houseplant.

"How do you know this guy?" Antonia asks me. "Is he one of your golfing buddies?"

My face cracks with disbelief. *"I don't golf."*

"Really? I figured you would," she says. "This better not suck like the last music thing you coerced me into attending."

Six months ago, I convinced Antonia to be my plus-one for a concert I was reviewing by a British singer-songwriter whose songs all seem to be about eating warm buns while waiting for a ferry. As retribution, I was forced to sit with her through the Julia Child biopic that was screening that summer.

Kulwant gets onstage accompanied by his detuned Tele-caster and a woman with kohl-smeared eyes holding a violin but standing behind a drum set. At first, the underwater notes he picks on his guitar, played to no discernible rhythm, sound intentionally unpleasant. The violinist begins to play a swirling figure as the guitar's chord pattern begins to shift. Kulwant, in a dark button-up shirt, steps to the microphone and closes his eyes.

His voice is gravelly and Springsteen-ish. The song is stirring but perhaps too simple, and yet Kulwant's mere presence holds the attention of everyone in the room.

"He's not bad," Antonia says, as Kulwant changes guitars between songs. "How do you know the guy?"

"We're old friends," I ask.

"But all your other friends are so horrible."

"I've been hiding him from you. I wasn't sure you were worthy."

"He's cute, too."

Something inside her purse blips. She reaches for her iPhone for the fifth time that evening.

"Who are you texting?" I ask.

"Some guy from Craigslist who wants to buy my van," she says. "But he keeps flaking out on me about the price. At this point, I'm willing to give it away."

KULWANT AND I both realize we'll never be as close as we once were. He's still the accidental horseman and artist; and I'm a writer hot for a big score. Our views on ambition and glory put us in rival churches.

In an effort to win a convert, Kulwant convinces me to accompany him to the Fraser Valley Auctions, which happens to be held on the same Sunday as the B.C. Derby. Only a fifteen-minute drive away from the equestrian facility where the yearlings were sold, this auction house sells livestock such as cattle, chicken, sheep, goats, and rabbits. Every four months, it also takes bids on previously owned horses. If the yearling auction is like a new-car dealership, this place is a junkyard sale, where people sift through cast-off animals for bargains.

"It's not a given these horses will be turned into dog food, right?" I ask Kulwant on the highway. "Some of them can be retrained, right?"

"I called the auction house this morning," he says. "I asked the person who answered what kind of horses they sold there. 'All kinds of them,' the guy said. And then I asked him what happens to the horses. And he told me, 'All kinds of things.'"

The auction house has a quaint, frontier-style facade connected to a low-slung holding barn with a corrugated aluminum roof. We pass through the entrance into a kitchenette that serves hamburgers and sliced hot dogs on hamburger buns. A cook behind the counter directs us to a door in the back.

We find ourselves in a cramped, windowless room with a thick band of yellowing caulk smeared on the walls below the ceiling; it's as though someone were trying to hold the building together with Krazy Glue. Around us on steeply tiered benches that descend from one corner are guys in cowboy hats, mothers with their kids, and young couples. In the other is a fenced-off dirt floor. Flies plump as coat buttons circle in the air. By the fence at the foot of the benches, a woman sits cross-legged on the floor with her baby in a car seat.

Behind the fence, a door opens and a young woman in a cowboy hat and a windbreaker rides in on a chestnut-coloured horse with an orange tag on her hip.

"The next horse we have is Alicia," says the auctioneer, whose delivery is slightly more percussive than the one at the yearling auction. "She's a six-year-old mare. She'd be great for trail riding. She has received thirty days of professional training."

She goes for $500. Bidders eyeball the horses like the audience in last week's auction, only this time they're looking for meat and not conformation. They hold up blue cards when a horse captures their fancy. Four thoroughbreds are spat out of the door, a mare and three geldings that have only been halter-broken and are being sold as lot. They bobble against each other as they circle the pen. All four of them go for $400.

While horses occupy an awkward space between pet and livestock in the U.S. and Canada, the slaughter of horses, including those sent from the States, is only permitted north of the border. Some of the meat from these animals is sent to countries like France and Japan, where it is prized for its sweet flavour and low fat content; colts and geldings provide the most delectable meat.

Many racehorses, which have been bred to be ornery and high-strung, can't be converted into jumpers or trail horses no matter how hard an organization like New Stride tries. After they have dropped to the lowest class and travelled to the smallest tracks, there's no place left for them. Given the medications and hormones that racehorses get, slaughtered thoroughbreds are often turned into dog food or rendered into products like crayons and lubricants.

Randi is still horrified by the memory of inadvertently helping a friend prepare a bow-legged horse for a meat auction. "He
was hard to control, but he always liked me," she told me earlier
that year. "I give the guy driving the truck the horse's papers. He
goes, 'He's not going to need papers where he's going.' When I
saw his little nose in the trailer window, I started fucking crying.
I'll never forget that. Now when people take horses from me, I
always ask them for some money. There'll be people who'll say I
want a horse, they'll bring their kids, and then they'll bring them
to an auction and collect five hundred bucks. If you get some
money from them up front, then you know they aren't doing that."

Despite these oppressive surroundings, the crowd has the
same optimistic tone as the yearling sale. The bidding for a
fifteen-year-old white draught horse that spent years pulling
a carriage around Stanley Park grows over $1,000. "Come on,
folks," says the announcer. "Here's a horse you can ride at night.
A horse that's so big you can survive a collision with a car." People chuckle nervously.

The woman who eventually claims the horse gives her friends
that look of self-amazement you exude when you've talked yourself into a big-ticket purchase.

Standing out in my chunky, plastic-framed glasses and cashmere sweater, I am ill at ease. Why? Is it because I'm not yet
desensitized to the horror I'm witnessing, or is it a sentimental
reaction? I believe it's the latter, but when a skinny young yearling, almost deer-like in her build, is sold for $60, I pull aside
Kulwant to leave.

"You see what I mean?" asks Kulwant, who has watched the
auction in grave silence, as we step into my car.

I'm not yet sure what the point of our visit was, if it wasn't
only to depress me. No one at the auction looked to me like a
dead-eyed horsemeat merchant. Horse people are farm people,
who love animals, just not any one animal. And while it's worth

supporting rescue groups like New Stride, even the slaughter of horses makes sense when the alternative is to abandon the animals in a field to starve to death.

We get to Hastings in time for the B.C. Derby, the province's most lucrative competition of the year. This year, the Grade III stakes race belongs to Winning Machine, an out-of-town horse from Seattle who edges out Jersey Town, another "shipper" from New York. Local favourite Tommy Danzigger fades in the lane and finishes seventh.

I'm glad to be here, around horses that have travelled a long way from their first auction—with time to go before the next one.

AFTER A WEEK of rain, Blackie's next race occurs on a clear and crisp day. The late-afternoon sunlight, which was washed out like a lager through the summer, now has the depth and richness of a pale ale.

After my argument with Randi, I decide to avoid her today, lingering by the paddock fence as I watch her speaking with Fernando Perez.

The night before the race, Carole Serene sends me the transcript of her first communication with my horse. "She's an open book, she is," she tells me in an accompanying email. "While I didn't set out to help you with your 'wagering,' Blackie has divulged exactly how she will run based upon her position in the pack. Strategy can be worked out so that her rider gets her to the front early, a place she will endeavour to keep herself in for the full race."

After the opening preamble with Seth, Carole speaks with Blackie. She asks her whether her hock was hurting, as Randi had suspected earlier in the year. Like Sylvester, Blackie speaks with a slightly formal voice reminiscent, perhaps, of an exchange student from Scandinavia or the computerized voice of Stephen Hawking:

BLACKIE: Oh yes, but that is not a sore hock anymore—it seems to be well now.

CAROLE SERENE: Do you like racing, Blackie?

BLACKIE: Oh, enough I guess.

CAROLE SERENE: Do you want to be the fastest horse in the race?

BLACKIE: Doesn't matter.

CAROLE SERENE: Oh, you don't care if you win or not?

BLACKIE: Well, for me to win is to finish and get back to my house and eat and not have pain. That is my winning.

CAROLE SERENE: Blackie, Kevin and Randi tell me that you fade at the end of the race sometimes, and they ask if you do this because you are tired, or maybe you are sore. Can you tell me about that?

BLACKIE: Fade?

CAROLE SERENE: Yes, to go slower.

BLACKIE: Oh, well it just doesn't matter so much if I'm not at the front of the group; then I know I will be at the back or the middle, so it won't make me faster or able to get to the front, so it really doesn't matter then.

CAROLE SERENE: So you stop trying?

BLACKIE: Looks like it.

CAROLE SERENE: What has to happen for you to try harder to be at the front of the horses and maybe come first or second?

BLACKIE: I like to run in the front of the group—if I can get there early I will try to stay there, but if I don't, well it just doesn't matter anymore.

Blackie's lackadaisical response is disappointing and alarming.

CAROLE SERENE: Does your rider ask you to wait before you go really fast, instead of starting really fast?

BLACKIE: Seems like it. When there's a big crowd of horses at the beginning we seem to wait for them to thin out before heading for the front—too late.

CAROLE SERENE: So you don't mind pushing through the thick crowd of horses at the beginning of the race?

BLACKIE: Not at all—I can do that, you know—I'm a big girl!

In the races she's run, with the possible exception of her most recent start, Blackie isn't normally too far from the front, nor does it make sense for her to go all out in the beginning. I begin to feel there must be static on the spiritual line between the horse and medium.

CAROLE SERENE: Do you like to meet the people Kevin brings to see you?

BLACKIE: Oh yes and they bring treats too—this is good—Kevin treats me nice.

CAROLE SERENE: Is there anything you want to tell Randi or Kevin now?

BLACKIE: Hello.

This part does please me. I want to believe she knows and likes me. Faith in this transcript: restored!

I'M AT THE fence when the race begins. Blackie breaks well, taking the lead and hugging the rail, while a 15-to-1 long shot called Sheisrough also races up ahead. Midway up the backstretch, Beautiful Breeze, the horse that won Blackie's last race, makes her move and passes Blackie. At the top of the lane, Beautiful Breeze overtakes Sheisrough, though both are far ahead of my horse, who fades, but still hangs onto third. As with the previous race, she just doesn't have enough luck or talent today.

Lingering by the rail when Perez dismounts, I see how hard Blackie is breathing, the sweat that coats her shanks, the dirt splattered on her front quarters. This time when I watch her I see thoroughbreds as the brittle creatures they really are— running backs with ski poles for legs. *For me to win is to finish and get back to my house and eat and not have pain. That is my winning.* Watching Blackie now, I have no doubt that Carole Serene knows a horse's heart.

I also watch her with the image of the slaughter auction in mind. Who was I to think there was nothing at stake in a claiming race? If a big-time horse rides for glamour and prestige, then the claiming horse rides for her life. If she doesn't win enough races and earn enough money, she faces eviction from her stall.

Randi, who yells at and defends her animals with equal ferocity, had every reason to be angry with me. To believe that thoroughbreds live to race doesn't mean one should discount the effort and strain involved in their work. I took that for granted. A horse like Blackie, not the most gifted runner, could easily give up against stronger competition, and yet she keeps herself in every race. She races for her life, but she also races for Randi. And through Randi, she races for me. How could I think I deserved better?

I take my time before heading to the backside. When I get there, the horses who've raced that day have all been walked and fed and the shed row is empty. From her stall, Blackie has a sleepy expression on her face, but her ears prick up when she sees me.

"That was such a good race," I tell her, placing a hand on her neck. My voice cracks and I'm glad there's no one around to see this. "You ran so well. I am so proud of you, and I'm so glad you didn't hurt yourself. You've never disappointed me. I'm so glad I've known you. You need to know that, okay?"

Blackie pops her head and nips my blazer, looking for a treat. "Hey, I just got that dry-cleaned."

It's still not clear whether Blackie likes me, but the more I think about it, the more it becomes irrelevant. Maybe wanting a horse to love you is like wanting your favourite song to be written about you, wanting the narrator of your favourite book to be your best friend: a fanciful notion, a wholly unnecessary one. What's really important is how much you love that animal, and how loving an animal changes you.

I lean up against the stall gate and wrap my hands around the horse's neck. A horse's neck is all muscle, a hidebound tree trunk. Hugging a horse reminds you of how it felt to cling onto a parent as a toddler.

"Don't die," I whisper to her. *"Don't ever die."*

"What's the matter with you?"

I turn to see Randi, looking tired, and sucking on another smoke.

"I'm drunk," I lie. "I get this way when I'm drinking."

"You're funny," she says.

➔ 17 ⬅

BEWARE THE MARE!

THE CITY IS easing into its damp, cold, and unremittingly grey back half. It rains all morning, and though it stops by the time we get to Blackie's next race, the racing oval resembles oatmeal streaked with brown sugar.

I catch Randi in the paddock watching Blackie—whose tail is braided in a series of knots, to keep it from sticking to her legs in the slop—as she's being walked around by Alex's son, Shawn. "Where's your entourage?" she asks me.

For the first time in months, I've come unaccompanied to watch my horse race. "Everyone's afraid of the rain," I tell her on the paddock's grassy island. "They're all chickenshit."

Fernando Perez, our rider, approaches us. "My only instruction to you," Randi says, "is to win. Just win."

After competing in open claiming races since her first win, Mocha Time—who's racing tenth out of the gate—has finally gotten into a conditional race against horses at her price that haven't triumphed more than once this season. That means she won't be facing many of the tougher horses that have beaten her this season, like Beautiful Breeze and Sultry Eyes. All the handicappers in the *Form* have her pegged to win, the punter's kiss of death, and when the horses are loaded in the gates she's paying the least at 2-to-1.

After parting with my cash at the betting window, I spot Randi at the stairwell landing that leads to the owners' boxes.

"THERE THEY GO," says track announcer Dan Jukich. "THEY ALL COME AWAY WELL. GRAYROSS GAL, QUICKENS TO THE EARLY LEAD. HERE'S MOCHA TIME AND BAMBOO DIVA MOVING IN."

Blackie draws in from the outside to get to the head of the race in the opening furlong, which takes up a lot of her energy. The race passes us, the thumping of the hooves is heavier in the rain—like a boxer's blows landing on a heavy bag in the gym.

Randi's upset that Blackie isn't closer to the rail at the turn. "And now you're like three wide," she says, cursing the horse. "Don't be a retard."

Still, Blackie is in second after a fast first quarter, three-quarters of a length behind a 70-to-1 shot named Grace's Star.

This time, luck is on our side. Midway through the back-stretch, Grayross Gal, the classy nine-year-old, tries to make her move but is hemmed at the rail by the long shots that are racing up front. Grace's Star begins to fade and Blackie takes the lead by the far turn.

"Come on, Blackie!" Randi screams. "Get ahead by the lane. Keep fucking riding that fucking thing, she'll stop on you," she yells at Perez. "Come on, keep moving."

Blackie builds her lead to two turns by the lane, but by this point a lane opens up inside for Grayross Gal, who starts gaining on Blackie, as do Mozambique, McGill, and Kachina Dream. Blackie is moving at full power, her ears pinned back, nostrils flared to suck the damp air into her partially obstructed lungs; Perez urges her along, accentuating her strides with every morsel of his strength. And yet it might not be enough. It's going to be another narrowly avoided victory.

A few hardy railbirds rush into the empty apron to catch the stampede to the wire, like ants descending on a discarded sandwich. Randi is flipping out: "NOOOOOOO!"

"THEY'RE CLOSING IN ON MOCHA TIME," Jukich says, before taking in a quick breath. "SHE'S LOOKING FOR WIRE..."

The photo sign lights up, which we take to mean that the winner is under review. Randi's pessimism clings to me like lint, and I know for certain the horse has lost again. Climbing down the stairs to the track, we see the number nine, Blackie's number, appear next to the first-place sign. The photo sign is up because second, third, and fourth places are the only positions that still need to be sorted out.

"She won!" I yelp.

"Oh good," Randi says flatly. "She's a cocksucker. Fucking thing stops like nobody's business."

We step into the winner's platform. Maybe I deserve being here without my entourage, given my earlier arrogance. I shake hands with Shawn, who is grinning as though he rode the horse himself to score. "I was like, this thing's gonna come off the rail and get her as usual," he says, referring to Grayross Gal.

"Did you have money on this race?" I ask him.

Shawn lowers his eyes, and his expression suddenly hazes over with guilt. "I quit betting," he admits. "Don't tell my dad. It'll break his heart."

I promise not to say a word.

AFTER THE RACE, I go home and put together my notes for Harris's novel, which I've spent the past week reading as meticulously as possible. We haven't spoken in over a month, and I'm not sure this gesture will be enough; I might be required to buy him lunch as well.

It takes two days to hear back from him, and that's only because he needs a ride from the doctor's office. The clinic where his vasectomy is performed turns out to be only a block from my house. I find Harris standing outside the medical building, his face red and bloated like a water balloon, almost as though he's been crying. I open the door for him as he waddles to the car.

"I've been waiting half an hour," he says impatiently, when he's inside. "Why didn't you answer your phone?"

"I forgot to turn the ringer back on," I say, pulling into traffic. "You said it would take an hour."

"Well, I was wrong," he says, biting his lip.

Harris, who sits in my car turned on one hip, doesn't want to go home right away. On his recommendation, we stop at the favourite eatery of his childhood: the Tomahawk Restaurant, a throwback burger joint stuffed with kitschy Aboriginal knick-knacks that serves insanely overstuffed burgers. As it's a weekday, we have little trouble getting a table and each order a Skookum Chief: a hamburger topped with cheddar, round-cut bacon, sliced hot dog, tomato, and fried egg.

Our burgers arrive during an extended trip that Harris makes to the restroom. I wait a couple minutes before I take on my Skookum Chief, which is surprisingly ergonomic for a burger with so many works—the fried egg, which I had thought was over-the-top, in fact makes for a good binding agent.

"What took so long?" I ask, adjusting the cardboard Native headdress on my head.

"My balls."

"Sorry, of course."

"They're *delicate*," he says, picking at his yam fries. "They're in a bandage and secured in a jock, and well, I wanted to see how it was all held together and put some lavender oil on them."

"Lavender oil?" I ask.

"It's supposed to reduce the swelling."

I drop my burger on my plate and start snickering. "I'm sorry," I say.

"It's not funny."

"I know."

Harris, in fact, starts crying. At first he tries to fight it off. Soon, the tears tumble down his face and his shoulders begin to heave. "You don't know how painful this is," he says, after he's calmed down enough to mop his eyes with a napkin. "All that tugging down there—it was like I was getting a root canal in my scrotum. Complications often arise from these procedures. What if I am in genital discomfort for the rest of my life?"

"Calm down."

He glares at me through his moistened eyes. "You won't know how it feels until it happens to you."

"It will *never* happen to me."

"See, you're smug."

"Look, I didn't mean to make fun of you. And I'm sorry again that I let you down. I look at your life all the time and I feel like a failure."

"Did you really like my novel?"

"Yeah," I say. "Especially the first half."

I let him quiz me about his manuscript, and I clarify the thoughts I offered earlier by email. And then we order coffee and chatter on about other things in our lives, the books we're reading, the whereabouts of mutual friends. While I have other errands that day, I sense that Harris doesn't want to be alone, parsing his bits, so we make conversation the way we used to, when the majority of our twenties still spooled ahead of us.

We talk about how fluorescent light bulbs are depressing; how if we were women, both of us would choose "sexy cat" as our Halloween outfit; how baby urine comes to mind whenever we drink apple juice.

After our second refill, a server places a bill on the table between us. Harris stares at it like a cat standing over a mouse he's pawed to death. I drag the receipt towards me.

"You're forgiven," he says.

⤳ 18 ⟅

THE BEST OF COMPANY

Anne MacLennan, who makes silks, saddle towels, helmet covers, and blinkers for horsemen at Hastings and Woodbine, has been involved in racing for three decades. She's managed breeding farms, galloped, and trained. After Bolulight, the horse she owned with her then-husband, won the B.C. Derby in 1991, they took their local champion down to Golden Gate Park for three years. As a Canadian, she could only work on her own horses; in her extra time, she volunteered with the woman running the Golden Gate silks shop and learned enough about the trade to start her own business, which now employs two other women, in Vancouver.

I've commissioned her to design my own personalized silks for Blackie's final race this season. It's only just occurred to me that I could dress up a jockey according to my whim.

"Bright, contrasting colours are the best," she tells me in her apartment as she looks over the crudely drawn sketch I've made with felt-tip pens. "Tasteful earth tones don't work because they blend with the scenery."

"What if I wanted to put boobs on them?" I ask, thinking strictly in theoretical terms. "What if I wanted really firm, perky boobs?"

"You probably can. I've had people ask me if you could put marijuana leaves on their silk."

Jockey silks are too important for boobs or weed. I'm designing my own flag or coat of arms, not a souvenir shot glass or a set of big-wheel mud flaps. The silks are my own personal stamp on my horse; the more it says about me, the more it will be as though a part of myself is on the horse as she races.

What a set of silks should actually convey are the things you value. In my case, I feel that my silks, like a totem pole or a religious painting, should tell the story of my season at the track, when I first met Randi and Blackie. And so while my initials might appear in the silks, the black Gibson SG guitars, blue lightning bolt, and NASCAR-style black-and-white checks on the sleeve are a tribute to Blackie and Randi, who sings AC/DC's "Back in Black" to the horse when they walk. And the red and blue of the body remind me of the Rosie the Riveter poster you see on Randi's door. These are things that are special to me.

BLACKIE IS ENTERED in the ninth and last race today, but I arrive early to cheer Sylvester on in the fifth race. On the grassy island in the paddock, I watch Randi kiss her favourite horse on the neck. After she gives jockey Robert Skelly instructions for the race, I follow her to a spot on the apron near the finish line. It's a bright, albeit chilly, day.

"If he sucks in this race," Randi says gruffly, "he's going to be a show horse."

Skelly rides Sylvester up by the rail, which the horse doesn't like. "He won't go on the rail, he just won't," she says. "I forgot to tell Skelly, but I can't remember to tell everyone fucking everything." The horse has a tough trip, finishing fifth.

Afterwards, when she watches the replay, Randi points out where Sylvester is blocked as he tries to make his move. She seems both angry about Sylvester's bad luck and relieved that she has reason to believe that he can still race.

"I don't even want to fucking run Blackie," she says in the stable afterwards. "I'm just going to fucking scratch her."

I'm glad she decides otherwise, as I have friends and family coming down. Back in the frontside, I catch up with Harris, Angie and their kids. I suggest we go to the restaurant, where I've made a reservation for twelve.

"My parents and their friends are coming, too," I explain to Harris as we climb the stairs into Silks. "They were here the first time I won, so maybe they're lucky."

"Do they have long moles with hair growing out of them?" Liam asks me.

"What are you talking about?" I ask him.

There's an extra element of oddness to Liam today. While Jack is dressed in an age-appropriate T-shirt and cut-off jean shorts, Liam is wearing corduroys and a blazer. Despite Angie's repeated insistence that he stand straight, he's hunched over when I see him, too.

"Some Asian people grow hairs out of their moles for good luck," Liam says.

I turn to Angie and Harris. "Is that really true?" I ask them.

"Well, I would check with another source," Angie says to me. "Google it when you get home."

An Internet search later confirms this superstition.

The afternoon starts well. I pick the winner in the sixth; I pick the winner in the seventh but change my mind at the last moment and ask the cashier to change my bet to a horse that loses; and then I get the winner of the eighth.

"Why did you bet on that horse?" asks Liam, who has insisted on sitting next to me. "Is he the speed?"

"Uh-uh," I say. "He's a closer. There's too much speed, and none of it's any good."

While his brother, Jack, makes bubbles in his cola, Liam watches me examine the *Form*, then he turns to his own copy of the racing broadsheet, crossing out underlays—the bad-value bets.

"I shouldn't have cut my nails today," Harris says as we watch the seventh race replay on the TV screen at our table. "I have nothing to bite."

"We're not leaving with even our shirts," suggests Angie, whose husband only recently stopped complaining about his breached testicles.

Harris riffs off his wife's joke: *"I'll bet this sweater on five to win."*

My parents and their friends, friends of my father from the Rotary Club and their wives whom I've known for at least two decades, show up fifteen minutes later. They introduce themselves to Harris and his family. We watch as Fernando Perez appears in the television monitor wearing my new blue-and-red silks. My dad, in his checked sports jacket, is in high spirits and even willing to put some money on my horse.

"A cook who used to work for me saw you here the other day," he says to me. "He wasn't sure he should tell me, because he thought you might have a habit."

"If the horse wins," I say, "I'll buy your next set of winter tires."

He nods. "It's a deal."

Now that Blackie's back in an open claiming race, she's no longer a favourite, running at 6-to-1 behind favourites like Beautiful Breeze, Sultry Eyes, and Quickens. The gates open and Blackie, racing out of gate number four, breaks well and takes the lead by the turn. She hasn't been the early front-runner much this season, and when she runs the first quarter at a zippy time of 22.48, followed closely by Quickens, I worry that she'll fade.

We get up from our tables and begin cheering and shouting. For the first time this season, I am no longer cheering for my glory or my wager but for my horse; I'm no longer cheering for a win, but a safe finish. Your horse's only job is to run. It's your responsibility to love her. Your job is to show your appreciation for an animal who lets you live through her; who allows you to claim her determination, class, and grace as your own; who's there for you to forget, momentarily, the muddle you've made of your life, your own awful way of going—your own sore spots and bad trips.

Midway through the backstretch, Quickens overtakes Mocha Time from two out, and I begin to think that she's already used up her best. But Blackie seems even more determined than usual. Perhaps she knows the season is closing in and that there's no reason to reserve her strength; perhaps she just feels good today; perhaps she woke up today and decided she wanted to come first.

For whatever reason, she refuses to give up ground, and the two horses run neck and neck at the turn and then the home stretch. In that flash of red and blue silk that we spot from the distance, I see myself and the year that's passed so quickly.

Now I know Blackie will win. She can do it, everyone thinks she can do it, she's about to do it, she almost does, but then Quickens prevails by a neck.

IT WOULD HAVE been nice to have that winner's photo, but most of us make money from our bets anyway, and we leave happy. My parents invite me and Harris's family to dinner at a Chinese restaurant, but the kids want to feed carrots to the horse, so we decline. The track is already starting to empty by the time we leave for the barn. Jack and Liam stroll ahead, Liam still stooped over as he walks.

"If you're going to be Liam's role model," Angie says, "I wish you would improve your posture."

I throw my shoulders back and straighten out my spine. "What do you mean?" I ask.

"You don't see it?" Harris says. "Liam wants to be like you when he grows up. Not *me*, the guy who puts a roof over his head, but *you*."

I can't resist gloating.

"So that's why he's wearing the blazer?" I ask. "And that's why he's slouching?"

Angie nods. "He's going to have to save his birthday money if he wants to buy his own horse."

Liam is standing by the paddock fence, staring at his copy of the *Form* as though the races are still underway. He doesn't look like me. To my eyes, he's copying some of the railbirds here, the guys who seem to have been born with a neck wattle and a prescription for Lipitor.

"It's just a phase," I say. "He'll grow out of it."

"He's an oddball," Harris tells me, "but there are worse people for him to be like. There are rapists, for example."

That night, I go home and take down my to-do list.

1. ~~BECOME A HOME OWNER~~ BOUGHT A RACEHORSE
2. ~~FIND TRUE LOVE~~ VISITED A BREEDING SHED
3. SETTLE DOWN & START A FAMILY
4. ~~SEE THE WORLD~~ VISITED SARATOGA
5. ~~LEARN ANOTHER LANGUAGE~~ TALKED LIKE A RAILBIRD
6. ~~START A RETIREMENT PLAN~~ REDUCED GAMBLING
   LOSSES
7. ~~GET A TATTOO~~ SERIOUSLY CONSIDERED GETTING A
   TATTOO

Crossing out the last un-struck item, I write after it: "BECAME A FATHER FIGURE TO LIAM." And then I toss out the list.

I accomplished everything I wanted by *not* accomplishing those things. Instead I bought a racehorse. From her example, I come to see persistence as its own success. You might win some and lose others, but you prove yourself every time you run honestly.

THE LAST TIME I see Blackie is January, when Aki and I make a six-hour drive to Portland to watch her run in a mid-week sprint. Because the horse ran so well that summer, another trainer convinced Randi to ship her horse south for the winter rather than turn her out to a farm for the off-season. When she sees me, Blackie, who's had a tough season adjusting to her new home, nips my collar looking for treats. Aki and I both insist that it's our presence, a mini-reunion with familiar humanoids, that pushes her into a second-place finish that afternoon.

By early April, Blackie is due to be sent back to Vancouver for the start of the Hastings meet, where she won $22,707 the year before, but the Portland trainer decides to enter her in one last race. In that race, Blackie is claimed. I want to claim her back when she races again, but Randi, who owned the bulk of the horse through the winter, says she can't afford it.

I don't want to overstate the loss of the horse. Claiming horses come and go. But I do feel as though a wonderful period in my life has passed. In the end, I get what I originally wanted— to own a racehorse for only a year. In all my life, it has never sucked more to get what I want.

When the racing season starts up again, I'm still not sure what to do. Nick hasn't been quick to return the money I gave him earlier; the cheque I gave him went to another trainer in Portland, who had access to Mocha Time's account and cleaned it out. She blamed her misfortune on a client who stiffed her for an even-bigger bunch of money. And so it goes.

With that outstanding cash, I could reinvest in another of Randi's horses. While I'm back at the track, I catch up with familiar faces. Sylvester starts the season as a pony horse, but finishes second in a race that September. Riley, who's become enormous over the winter, runs for the first time—and finishes dead last—later in the season before being given away to be a trail horse. I also meet new horses like Twobit'n Billie, who won three times at three different distances, and other winners like Macondo and Cry Cry Cry. Aubrey Road, also known as the Girl, is retired from racing to become a broodmare; her first foal is due the next spring. I follow Blackie's race results online as she runs and loses at county fairs across Oregon.

On one race day, I see Sid Martin, who tells me he's done what he swore, months earlier, he'd never do—retire. (Martin would die of cancer the following year, in 2011, at age 82.) That same afternoon, I see Chad Hoverson, who has set aside any plans to quit riding, saddling up in the paddock. My friend Kulwant, however, has quit his job at Hastings. He's in Mexico, working on an organic farm and living out of the van he purchased from Antonia. (Despite her original, cautious attraction, Antonia later decided Kulwant was not her type. He remains proudly single, and she's dating a local political blogger.)

Near the end of the summer, Alex is found dead from a heart attack by a security guard at the harness track in Cloverdale. Randi cries when she learns the news. "Shawn is still working here, but he looks like a lost soul," she tells me in the summer. "I'm going to try to look out for him. His dad was all the family he had." When she brushes Sylvester, she sings the songs Alex made up for him.

In 2011, I take the money still owed to me and put it into the almost gibbled little dude—Freddy—who will start running as a two-year-old in the fall. "He's not gibbled anymore," Randi says. "He's a friendly little thing, but he's kind of high-strung. A dink. I'm hoping he will be a runner."

"Do you think I can walk him around the shed row someday?"

"Maybe. He'll have to get his nuts out first."

A FEW MONTHS before Alex's death that spring, I rejoin Randi on her route. It hasn't gotten hot, so it isn't yet unpleasant. I follow her to the back-fence gate of one house to greet an old Rottweiler with watery blue eyes named Bosco. "I haven't seen you in so long, Bosco," she coos. "Did you miss me?" The dog yelps as he gobbles up the biscuits Randi throws at him. "I'll give you a couple more since I haven't seen you in months."

"I like Bosco," I say.

"I hadn't seen him in a while. I was worried he might have died. Did you see the way he walked?"

"Um, yeah," I say, thinking how he tottered creakily, like my parents' nine-year-old Labrador.

To a point, I've missed Randi's mail route. I feel as though she wants me around; I like that. That said, if it starts raining, I'll definitely bail.

"Listen," Randi says as she unlocks a grey storage box and loads her satchels with mail for the next segment of her route, "I feel really bad you lost Blackie. I know you loved that thing. I did, too."

"It's okay."

"Last year might have been one of my worst seasons. What with all those people not paying me, it's no fun being in the hole."

"It wasn't that bad, was it?"

"It wasn't *entirely* bad. Don't put fucking words in my mouth."

As we cross the street, a man walking a small dog calls out Randi's name.

"I haven't seen you for a while," he says. "What happened—the horses not winning?"

"No," she says, as she throws a biscuit to the dog, a chihuahua-pug mixture. "I just have to work."

"So, I programmed my pedometer to my stride," he announces. "I walk 8,064 steps. Six miles."

Randi turns to me. "We're always arguing over who walks more every day," she explains to me. She turns back to the guy with the lapdog: "You don't understand that I have to walk into the houses and up the steps."

The guy narrows his eyes as he works that into his calculation. "That might add, *oh*, another half a mile to your walk," he tells us.

"Let me show you," Randi says. She starts walking heel to toe in a line, like a tightrope walker, from the sidewalk to the front door of a house, and then to the next house. "It's almost the same distance from the sidewalk to the door as it is from one house to the next."

"Well," the guy says. "It looks like you'd pass a drunk-driving test."

The two of us, plus the dog, follow Randi through the rest of her route, up and down Venables and Adanac. The guy with the dog tells me he's never been to the track. He doesn't like to gamble, he says. When he explains that he has the largest cigar-band collection in the world, I feign amazement. (No, he doesn't even smoke the cigars.)

I wonder what people make of this little parade. And then a guy steps out of a truck and calls out to Randi. "My father was a postie," he tells her. "Dogs would follow him on his route, but never people."

Randi laughs. "It's not so bad when I have people with me," she says to us as we trail her down the block. "This is like visiting."

I feel the first drop of rain smudge my nose but change my mind about deserting her. I keep on walking.

AUTHOR'S NOTE

THE MATERIAL RELATING to Mocha Time and the racetrack can be verified online through various racing websites. While this book is non-fiction, I took some creative licence by conflating, making into composite characters, and changing names and distinguishing characteristics of friends and acquaintances. I did this as a way of protecting the privacy of others and sheltering myself from their anger. I've also exaggerated situations, occasionally, for comic effect; given myself the best one-liners in conversations; shuffled the chronological deck on some non-racing events; and thrown in one or two meaningfully traumatic experiences that actually occurred outside my year at the track.

ACKNOWLEDGEMENTS

At Hastings, I'd like to thank Rosann Anderson, Meesoo Lee, Dan Jukich, Aki Otomo, Paul Mabbott, Marlo Dunn, Raj Mutti, Sid Martin, Chad Hoverson, Anne MacLennan, Tommy Wolski, and Horatio Kemeny.

Outside of the track, I'd also like to thank Maya Wilson, Anne McDermid, Michelle Furbacher, Martha Magor, Carole Serene, Wynn Allbury, Derek Fairbridge, Rob Sanders, and Peter Norman.